HOUSING SECURITY

A SECTION 8 MEMOIR

CAROL LAMBERG

ISBN: 978-64314-580-8 (Paperback)
        978-64314-581-5 (Hardback)
        978-64314-582-2 (E-book)

 AUTHORS PRESS

AuthorsPress
California, USA
www.authorspress.com

ACKNOWLEDGMENTS

Thanks to Alexandra Kramskaya for the design of the cover art.

Thanks to my partner, Don Pfaff, for encouragement and creative nagging

Thanks to Chuck Edson for giving me thirteen years worth of the newsletter, "Housing Development Reporter," a most valuable gift. Thanks to Professor Roderick Hills for access to the NYU Law Library

Thanks to the individuals who spoke with me about their experiences:

Conrad Egan, Chuck Edson, Rick Gentry, Robert Elliot, Mark Willis, Ingrid Gould Ellen, Douglas Rice, Ronay Menschel, Allan Mallach, John Kelly, Elizabeth Holtzman, Alan Wiener, Carla A. Hills, Anthony Freedman, Nick Lembo, Mark Ginsberg, Michael Lappin, Vicki Been, Megan Sandel, Lauren Sandler, Donny Capa, Jeanne Dupont, Dan Rose, Barry Zigas, Joseph Ventrone, Jeff Brodsky, Richard Hunnings, Susan Cole, Stephan Russo, Kent Watkins, Robert Weiner, Fredrica Friedman, Tom Barbash, Marisa Rendanty, Mary Lou Westerfield

Thanks to Diane Yentel, Sarah Saadian and Ed Gramlich from the National Low Income Housing Coalition for referring me to tenants.

Thanks also to Steve Norman, Rhonda Rosenberg, Pam Taylor, Karen House, Linda Pratt and Pamela Talley from Kings County, Washington for referring me to tenants.

Thanks to Shalonda Rivers, Yanira Cortes, Geraldine Collins, Ramon and Denisse Cepada, Jane Terry, Maria Ventura and Jonay Palmer for telling me about direct experiences and sharing their knowledge with Section 8.

COMMENTS FROM EXPERTS

"Carol Lamberg was a key player in shaping what today we know as Section 8. Her mastery of housing policy led to important revisions in the 1974 legislation that led to greater social equity and opportunity for families. As interest builds in expanding Section 8 once again, there is still so much to learn from her about the best ways to promote and shape public policy."

Nicholas Dagen Bloom
Professor of Urban Policy and Planning
Director, Master in Urban Planning Program
http://www.hunterurban.org/faculty/nicholas-dagen-bloom

"Carol Lamberg has been a leader in affordable housing for decades. She was the executive director for the Settlement Housing Fund from 1983 until her retirement in 2014, where she helped to develop nearly 10,000 homes. No one knows more about the challenges of developing affordable housing, and no one understands the need for federal rental assistance better than Carol. Her new book about the Section 8 program is a must-read for anyone who wants to understand the program and the critical role it plays in providing stable, affordable housing for low-income families and individuals in need."

Ingrid Gould Ellen
Paulette Goddard Professor of Urban Policy and Planning
Director for Furman Center for Real Estate and Urban Policy
New York University
ingrid.ellen@nyu.edu

"If the COVID pandemic has taught us anything, it should be how crucial safe and secure housing is for all Americans—and how vulnerable so many are to losing it or to spending way too much of their monthly earnings for rent. The emergency measures implemented in the recent crisis must inspire a permanent solution to the problem. Drawing on her deep experience with housing policy, Carol Lamberg makes a compelling case for how universal Section 8 rental assistance for all who qualify would fulfill the historical promise made in 1949 to provide "a decent home and a suitable living environment for every American family." This is an important book with an urgent message."

"Lizabeth Cohen, Harvard University, author of Saving America's Cities: Ed Logue and the Struggle to Renew Urban America in the Suburban Age"

Lizabeth Cohen
Harvard University Distinguished Service Professor
Howard Mumford Jones Professor of American Studies
Department of History Harvard University

"I met Carol Lamberg when I was Chief Legislative Assistant for Senator Jacob K. Javits of New York and Carol came to my office to lobby me to help get amendments to the FHA loan requirements so that more affordable housing could be built in higher cost areas like New York City. Carol was extremely knowledgeable and effective, and I spoke to Senator Javits about adding provisions to the upcoming housing legislation that would allow housing to be built in New York City under the FHA programs. The effort was successful and that was the start of a long collaboration between us in the cause of affordable housing. Carol has done so much in the cause of providing low and moderate income housing and has been so creative in going about this work, that this book should be something that anyone interested in this important issue must read."

Charles S. Warren
Partner and Chair, Environmental
Kramer Levin Naftalis & Frankel LLP
1177 Avenue of the Americas, New York, New York 10036
T 212.715.9387 F 212.715.8096
cwarren@kramerlevin.com

"Carol Lamberg has long been one of the country's most creative and effective champions of affordable housing, both as a developer and as an advocate. In "Housing Security: A Section 8 Memoir" Lamberg tells the story of the nation's largest and most flexible low-income housing subsidy program. She is uniquely positioned to tell this story, having successfully advocated for key provisions in the program's design and having used the program to develop a wide range of affordable housing projects. Drawing from personal experience, interviews with key figures in the program's design and development, and the public record, she discusses the program's origins, its accomplishments, its disappointments, and its potential to address the nation's housing affordability crisis. Brimming with insights, the book is essential reading for housing policy."

Alex Schwartz
Professor of Public and Urban Policy, The New School
Author of *Housing Policy in the United States* (Routledge, 2021)

CONTENTS

Chapter 1   Introduction 1

Chapter 2   Earlier Housing Programs 5

Chapter 3   The HUD Moratorium 19

Chapter 4   The Housing and Community
Development Act Of 1974 27

Chapter 5   Section 8 Success Launch 39

Chapter 6   Impoundment and the Budget 51

Chapter 7   Carla A. Hills 59

Chapter 8   Manhattan Plaza and Program Flexibility 69

Chapter 9   The Cost Conundrum 87

Chapter 10   Reaganomics and Dwindling
HUD Budgets 105

Chapter 11   What do Tenants Say? 115

Chapter 12   My Somewhat Humble Recommendations
for the Future 127

CHAPTER 1

Introduction

I AM AN UNABASHED supporter of Section 8, the Federal housing program that helps lower income families afford to pay their rent. As originally enacted in 1974, this was probably the most flexible, effective housing program in the history of federal housing programs over the past eighty years or so. Even today, the program assists 3.4 million families, many of whom might be homeless without the program. While the administration of the program is far from perfect, I wish we had more of it to complain about.

Section 8 could and should be expanded to help every American who cannot afford market rate housing, ranging from the very poor to middle income families and individuals. I would call the expanded program "Housing Security." It would look like the 1974 Act that established the program. However, it would be available for everyone who cannot afford the HUD established fair market rent for an appropriately sized apartment or house. I would also revive the Section 8 Program for New Construction and Substantial Rehabilitation. All it would take are a few amendments to the Housing Act and a vastly increased housing budget.

Many in the academic world and many advocates agree that rental housing assistance should be expanded. I also hear surprisingly positive opinions from other people who might seem less likely to express such a view.

One example is Donny Capa, a hairdresser at Rossi on West 56 Street in Manhattan. Like the owner of the salon, Donny lives in Staten Island. He shares his house with his wife, two sons and for many years he shared it with his mother. His family came from Albania. He is an avid gardener and likes to help his neighbors. He is especially generous when using his snow-blowing machine throughout his block during a blizzard. I asked Donny what he thought of the large shopping center and roller coaster planned for the area near the Staten Island ferry. He said that he will probably try it out, but his racist neighbors are somewhat negative. They say that only the "Section 8 people" will shop there. Then he told me that he had inherited three two-family houses from his father, and he loved it when he could rent to Section 8 tenants. "It's great. The Housing Authority pays me every month. I don't need to go to court. I had a lovely Black family for a few years. They were beautiful people—the best tenants I ever had. I wish I could find more Section 8 tenants."

I heard another unusual example of support from people who owned summer bungalows in Far Rockaway, Queens. During the financial crisis of 2008, an artist bought 13 bungalows at a very low price. He rents them to Section 8 tenants, mostly African Americans. The other owners live in Manhattan in the winters and use the bungalows on weekends or during summer vacations. The Manhattanites are delighted with their Section 8 neighbors. They live in the bungalows year-round and report problems to their neighbors and even take care of the problems. The neighbors are looking for ways to make Section 8 permanently available for the artist's bungalows.

Last but not exactly least was a report from the superintendent of a building that is partially assisted with Section 8. He told me that a few of the higher-income (market-rate) tenants said that they had been talking to one of the low-income tenants in the laundry room. The low-income tenant mentioned her Section 8 benefits. "Can we get some of that," asked the higher-income tenants.

This book describes the benefits of Section 8, a housing program that helps lower income tenants to pay their rent in privately owned buildings and in specific developments financed through the program. I begin by briefly describing some of the earlier programs, including early New York programs. Most federal programs started during the New Deal and others from the Great Society programs and the War on Poverty of the Johnson Administration. Next I discuss the original Section 8 legislation, enacted in 1974. I was fortunate enough to represent some of the New York groups that were advocating for affordable housing and was present when the bill was passed by the House of Representatives. The book will include interviews with lobbyists and former HUD officials who were there at the beginning. Ambassador Carla Hills, probably the best HUD Secretary in our history, is quoted and interviewed, as are others who helped her to achieve record high production levels. I include interviews with residents, developers, bankers and others who have used the program successfully.

I will provide a case study. I include Manhattan Plaza, a development on West 42 Street with 1688 apartments, mainly (70 per cent) for performing artists. This was one of the first projects to be subsidized with Section 8 in New York City. Section 8 prevented the project's bankruptcy in 1977, which would have had serious repercussions on the economic health of New York City, which had just started to recover from a fiscal crisis.

I will describe why the few failures were caused by unscrupulous developers, not the fault of the program. (The same could be said for public housing).

Angus Eaton, winner of the 2015 Nobel Prize in Economics, described extreme American poverty in an Op-ed article in the New York Times, January 24, 2018. He emphasizes the lack of decent shelter. "Indeed it is precisely the cost and difficulty of housing that makes for so much misery for so many Americans..."[1]

A wealthy country like the United States should be able to provide acceptable shelter for all its residents.

In Scotland affordable housing is a right. The same is true in Singapore, where 82 percent of the residents live in public housing, including many with beautiful architecture and amenities.

---

[1]   New York Times, January 25, 2018, page A27

How can we stand by and do nothing when people are literally living on the streets or where a middle-income family cannot find an affordable home within reasonable distance of work.

This shouldn't be.

CHAPTER 2

Earlier Housing Programs

THERE ARE MANY BOOKS and legal histories, some 1,500 pages or more, that chronicle the various American housing programs as they existed over time. I have read quite a few. I used to introduce myself as an expert on obsolete housing programs and legislation that never passes. This chapter is audacious enough to give a very short, selective history of government support for housing. Hopefully I will show how various programs and events led to the enactment of Section 8 in 1974.

It seems that New York City has always had a housing crisis. It's probably true of many areas of the country, but New York certainly has a well-documented history of housing problems. According to Richard Plunz in <u>A History of Housing in the New City</u>, the first government housing activity took place in 1624 when the Dutch West India Company established design controls. Of course, the rules were ignored, as were fire protection laws. Plunz describes how a fire in Chicago in 1871 stimulated thoughts in New York and elsewhere about how to design a large portion of a city.

Fast forward to 1890. Jacob Riis, a journalist and photographer, was an early housing pioneer. He decried a home consisting of one room, 12' by 12' inhabited by 5 families with 20 people. The furniture consisted of two beds. His famous book, <u>How the Other Half Lives</u>, contained multiple horror stories. His ethnic stereotypes are shocking, but his outrage about miserable housing is compelling. "The foul core of New York slums, home to tramp and rag-picker," appalls him, as does the fact that only 6 out of 24 tenements are "decent." His stories and photographs led to building codes and regulations to prevent overcrowding. He also attacks landlords who discriminated against the black families who migrated to New York after the Civil War, but claimed that fortunately, changes were occurring. In his chapter, "The Color Line in New York," he says that "there is no more clean and orderly community in New York than the new settlement of colored people that is growing up on the East Side from Yorkville to Harlem... Cleanliness is the characteristic of the negro in his new surroundings, as it was his virtue in the old." He believed that some landlords had recognized this positive tendency and were seeking Black tenants. Riis is much less kind to other ethnicities.

Jacob Riis sometimes sounds like one of today's housing advocates. He writes about the positive effects of housing on health and how better housing led to a reduced death rate. He makes a connection between housing and education. He criticizes the fact that different ethic groups do not live together in integrated buildings and neighborhoods. He praises the work of charitable organizations, the "silver lining" of the "black cloud." He would be pleased about the role of nonprofit organizations today in developing and operating high quality affordable housing. It would be great if current policy makers echoed the ideas of Jacob Riis, appreciating some of the excellent work being done today by community development organizations in cities and rural areas all across the United States. On the other hand, he vilifies greedy landlords. Today many landlords do excellent work, whereas there are some who certainly deserve Riis' bad rap.

Over the decades, New York's settlement house leaders, philanthropists, financial groups and politicians created programs to incentivize the development and operation of below market rate housing. Nicholas Dagen Bloom and Matthew Gordon Lasner describe these programs in their book, Affordable Housing in New York. The initial philanthropic efforts between 1870 and 1910 "yielded units for just 3,588 families, in a city with hundreds of thousands of tenement apartments." Still, many of the buildings are still standing. Some have been converted to high end uses, and others remain affordable. After World War I, New York and other cities passed rent control laws to deal with the housing "crisis." In New York City, the crisis keeps getting worse.

In 1936. James Ford, a Harvard professor, wrote an 838 page history called Slums and Housing. He quotes a 1929 Chicago study by Harvey Warren Zorbaugh as follows, "The slum is a bleak area of segregation of the sediment of society; an area of extreme poverty, tenements, ramshackle buildings, of eviction and evaded rents, an area of working mothers and children, of high birth rate, infant mortality, illegitimacy and death; an area of pawnshops and second-hand stores, of gangs, of 'flops,' where every bed is a vote." He does not mention homelessness, but everything else is still familiar. In a later chapter, he asked whether in 1936 there had been any progress at all. He claims that "Progress may be likened to mountain-climbing. There is a remote peak as an objective, but the path may wind and take a man over one knoll or minor eminence after another or through intervening valleys, before the ultimate ascent to the peak is possible. Housing reform is still among the foothills."

Although we have eliminated some of the worst conditions, we have a very long way to go. Some of us are impatient.

New York's Governor Alfred Smith realized that the government had to do something about housing. Tax abatement programs and low interest loans were the initial responses by New York State. One of the giant achievers in New York's housing history was Abraham Kazan, who initiated efforts by labor unions to create housing affordable to workers, mostly cooperatives. Kazan was a favorite of Robert Moses. The two indefatigable gentlemen "got things done." Kazan organized a mega-achieving nonprofit organization, United Housing Foundation, with the participation of many labor unions. United Housing Foundation produced thousands of cooperative units at a time, mostly during the 1950's and early 1960's.

Mr. Kazan did not suffer fools. Nor would he take "no" for an answer. He became famous and vaunted as would a corporate CEO today. Still, when he wanted the state housing agency to expedite an approval, he would go to Albany and sit for hours in the waiting room of the Commissioner's office until the Commissioner authorized the approval needed.

His last project was Coop City, a huge complex in the Bronx, consisting of over 15,000 apartments. There were construction issues, leadership problems and financial problems there for many years. However, the development is thriving decades later. After Mr. Kazan died in 1971 when construction costs were climbing, United Housing Foundation no longer plays as active a role in creating new housing.

Nicholas Dagan Bloom and Matthew Gordon Lasner in Affordable Housing in New York provide examples of developments using programs initiated between 1926 and 2014. Included were state supported public housing and buildings developed using the Mitchell Lama program, which created over 140,000 apartments between 1955 and the early 70's.

One could write additional volumes about early housing programs in New York. The one constant theme is that there have always been long waiting lists for all buildings.

Beginning with the Revenue Acts of 1856 and 1864, the federal government allowed individuals to deduct the interest expenses and local taxes connected with home ownership. However, the federal government did not become directly involved in housing until the 1930's, entering the arena as a way to end the great depression. At a conference in 1931, President Herbert Hoover was concerned because 50 per cent of all home mortgages were in default. There were "1,000 foreclosures per working day," between 1931 and 1932. At first programs consisted of measures to assist failing banks through purchases of mortgages by the federal government. Next in 1934, the Federal Housing Administration was created to insure mortgages, beginning with single-family homes and expanding over the decades to include rental housing, cooperatives, housing for the elderly, nursing homes, mobile home courts and urban renewal areas. According to the HUD website, 47.5 million homes and 48,500 multifamily buildings have been insured between 1934 and 2018. However, the accomplishments are blemished because of underwriting policies that involved "redlining," denying insurance to buildings in areas occupied by minorities.

Public housing had its conceptual start in 1934 when Secretary of the Interior, Harold L. Ickes established a Housing Division within the Public Works Administration. A memoir by Elizabeth Wood, a prominent housing leader from 1937 to the late sixties, describes the high quality of the residents and project design of the first public housing developments. In her book, "The Beautiful Beginnings, the Failure to Learn," she wrote about Chicago's Ida B. Wells development, which had the lowest median income of any project in the country. "The total unpaid rent for the first year of occupancy was $156.20. The tenants threw a party, collected the unpaid amount and handed it over to management." Elizabeth Wood was an advocate for careful tenant selection.

Also in 1934, the federal government started to create public housing for veterans. The Veterans Administration also offered loan guarantees for single family homes.

Between 1933 and 1937, 21,000 housing units were built in 35 cities by the Public Works Division, with little or no collaboration with localities. These public housing units mirrored the idealism of the New Deal. The federal agency staff studied the housing estates in Europe and garden city experiments in the United States. Buildings were created in a park like atmosphere with adjoining schools and other facilities. Design standards were high. Housing managers lived on site.

The studies that led to these early projects formed the basis for large scale development of public housing.

In 1937, the landmark Wagner-Steagall Act officially established public housing. One of the original purposes, as stated in the statute, was to encourage full employment after the depression. The federal government paid for capital costs. Local authorities selected the tenants, owned and managed the properties. The debate in Congress was harsh. Realtors preferred housing allowances for privately owned buildings. There was concern that the government would destroy free enterprise in real estate. Others were worried that the buildings would be too "nice" for low-income families, better than the housing available to middle income families. Therefore, in some cases very small rooms, closets with no doors and few amenities characterized many of the second wave of developments. Although public housing did not win architectural awards in New York City, the interior layouts were usually generous, with good light, air and utilities.

To the probable surprise of most housing advocates and New Yorkers today, Robert Moses cared about livable interior design for low income families. He especially wanted eat-in kitchens for families, but that was hard to achieve in New York. I was privileged to meet Mr. Moses when I was in college, writing my thesis on housing and urban renewal. I heard him talk about eat-in kitchens.

Although public housing had well-documented problems in Chicago and other parts of the country, the program was mostly successful in New York City until the late eighties and nineties, when federal government stopped providing enough money for repairs and operations. Over the years the problems have mounted, as has been widely publicized.

Originally public housing had many advantages. The federal government issued bonds to cover capital costs. Support for public housing was not subject to annual appropriations by Congress. (I wish we could arrange a similar advantage for Section 8 today). Local housing authorities owned and maintained the properties. Tenants paid only operating costs as rent. Still, in many localities the program was far from popular politically.

Beginning in 1946, similar programs were offered by the Department of Agriculture in rural areas.

A monumental act in 1949 provided funds for slum clearance and land acquisition. Local governments could condemn properties and sell them at a price that would allow feasible development. Two thirds of the price of land acquisition and demolition would be paid with federal funds. In New York, the State paid one sixth, and the locality paid the remaining sixth. In New York City, the going price attributed to sites after the urban renewal write down was $500 per housing unit. That land price enabled development on almost all of New York City's urban renewal sites. The policy lasted through the 1990's.

Most impressive was the goal of the 1949 Act: **"a decent home and a suitable living environment for every American family."** The Act authorized 810,000 additional public housing units and required that preference be given to those who were relocated because of redevelopment. Another less helpful provision required eviction from public housing of tenants whose income rose above legal limits.

In 2021 we are far from achieving the 1949 Act's goal. However, it might become possible if housing assistance became an entitlement, and enough money was provided to do the job well.

In 1954, renovation of older buildings became an allowable expense, when urban renewal was officially enacted as part of the federal tool kit. Although urban renewal has many critics, in New York it permitted site acquisition and write-down of the cost of land—valuable tools. Also in 1954, the Federal National Mortgage Association (Fannie Mae) was strengthened as a secondary market facility as well as a provider of "special assistance" for projects needing federal aid. (In 1968, Fannie Mae became privatized, although subject to government regulation).

In addition to public housing, the federal government initiated new loan programs over the years. In 1959, the Eisenhower administration started the Section 202 program for the elderly, when Congress overrode an initial veto. This was a direct loan program at prevailing interest rates for housing for people over 62 years of age. A similar program for families, the 221(d)(3) BMIR (below market rate interest) program, with 40 year loans at 3 per cent interest, followed in 1961 under the Kennedy Administration. Both programs required ownership by nonprofit organizations.

A program for profit-motivated organizations was also enacted, Section 221(d)(4), but this was basically a program to insure private multifamily mortgages. In many cases the income limits and per unit cost limits made it difficult to use these programs. Also in the 1961 Act, local Housing Authorities gained the right to allow families to remain in public housing after their incomes exceeded income limits, if they could not find adequate private housing. This resulted in a healthier income mix in many developments.

President Johnson created the Department of Housing and Urban Development (HUD) through the Housing Act of 1965. Previously most housing programs were administered by the Housing and Home Finance Agency. By granting cabinet status, housing 's importance supposedly became elevated. The first HUD Secretary was Robert Weaver, who had been the Administrator of the Housing and Home Finance Administration. He was also the first African American Secretary of any federal department. He was a public housing advocate and a believer in the ambitious goal of the Housing Act of 1949. Wendell Pritchett's biography of Robert Weaver provides an excellent history of housing programs in the sixties. ("Robert Clifton Weaver and the American City: The Life and Times of an Urban Reformer").

The Housing Act of 1965 also established the Rent Supplement Program, which allowed low income families to live in FHA financed apartments. However, in the first year no funds were appropriated for the program. Section 23 of the same act allowed local housing authorities to lease units in bond financed buildings and other private buildings to house low income families.

In 1966, I was working for the Department of Urban Affairs of Executive Council of the Episcopal Church. I organized a group of religious leaders, using a mailing list given to me by the staff. The list consisted of 500 Episcopal ministers, Bishops and Canons. I added the Josephite Fathers in the South, a client of my mentor, and a rabbi I knew from St. Louis, so we had a coalition of major religions to lobby for funds for the Rent Supplement program. I wrote their testimony for the hearings and still can remember the high quality of the questions and answers. That year (not necessarily cause and effect) $100 million were appropriated for the program. I was well coached by Harley Dirks, the head of the staff of the Senate Appropriations Committee.

Even more important, in 1966 the Model Cities Program was born, and originally called the "Demonstration Cities and Metropolitan Development Act."

The program was supposed to demonstrate the effectiveness of combining housing, social services, safety, employment training and other programs that would "improve the quality of urban life." It was initially planned that a few cities would be chosen. However, in order to get the program passed by Congress, appropriated funds had to be spread over cities throughout the country. Citizen participation was required. Still, this was an important part of President Johnson's War on Poverty. The death of Martin Luther King Jr. in 1968, the Black Power movement, the riots of the late sixties and the ambitious goals of the program did not generate a significant constituency to keep the program intact. However, the goals of the Model Cities Program resemble the best practices today of many nonprofit organizations in different areas of the country.

Two major initiatives occurred in 1968. The first was the Civil Rights Act, making it unlawful to discriminate in the sale, rental or financing of housing or in providing brokerage services. Over the years the law was amended to apply to other groups, including people with disabilities.

The second, the Housing and Urban Development Act of 1968, reaffirmed the goal of the 1949 Act to provide a decent home for all Americans. The 1968 Act was monumental. Congress determined that 26 million housing units could be built over the next decade, and the goal was to include six million for low-and moderate-income families. Two new production programs would help to achieve this goal. Section 235 provided subsidies to reduce interest rates to 1 per cent for single family homes for lower income families. Section 236 did the same for rental housing and cooperatives. Fannie Mae and the new Ginnie Mae (Government National Mortgage Association) were empowered to guarantee mortgages, including mortgage-backed securities. Prime rate was about 6.5 per cent in 1968. Income limits were set at 80 per cent of area median for both programs.

Subsidies were available for federally insured mortgages or for housing financed with municipal or state bonds. Because of lobbying efforts in which I was directly involved, up to forty per cent of the apartments in a Section 236 project became eligible for deeper subsidies, allowing an income mix. The federal government was set to expand its work, and the localities were enthusiastic about the potential. In New York, urban renewal sponsors were active as planners and advocates. The sponsors were neighborhood groups with a history of community involvement. Working closely with city officials, sponsors would decide in favor of public housing, or Section 236 or both in their communities.

In the sixties, Senator Edward Brooke from Massachusetts, the first African American member of the Senate, and others became worried about public housing. The concern was not about the condition, but rather the affordability. Very low-income families could not afford the rents, which had to pay for operating costs, which included payments in lieu of taxes. Hence, the Brooke Amendment was enacted in 1969. The amendment stipulated that tenants in public housing would not be required to pay more than 25 per cent of income for rent. The federal government would provide subsidies to cover operating costs. The federal government also established national income limits and cost limits, and these limits became a problem in New York City. The federal government's payments went up from $31 million in 1970 to $280 million in 1973.

At the same time in New York City, John Lindsay was Mayor and Simeon Golar became the Chairman of the New York City Housing Authority. Golar initiated policies to achieve racial integration in public housing. Welfare rights activists lobbied to assure that families receiving public assistance were not excluded from becoming tenants. Still, tenant selection guidelines were set to assure safety. In addition, the New York City Housing Authority had its own police force. Public housing in New York City was safer than buildings in the surrounding neighborhoods, as the public relations staff of the Authority liked to point out to the press.

In 1969 we achieved an amendment allowing Section 236 subsidies for part of a state or local bond-financed development, instead of an all-or-nothing approach. I lobbied for that amendment, a three-word beauty, "or part thereof." Because of my work with religious groups, I got to know the staff of the House and Senate housing subcommittees. I was working for a housing consultant, Roger Schafer. His clients included many religious institutions. At the request of state housing officials from New Jersey, we were able to insert the three-word amendment, "or part thereof," in the 1969 Act. HUD was opposed, worried that middle income tenants would resent or be reluctant to live with those who needed deeper subsidies.

After the amendment was included in the House bill, I asked the House staff counsel whether there had been a lot of debate as part of the committee discussions. The legislative mark up sessions excluded the public at that time. He told me that the two of us were the only ones who knew that the amendment was in the bill.

The goal of 600,000 affordable housing units in one year was never reached. In fact, Section 236 rental housing did not get into high production gear until 1969 when investors were able to obtain tax benefits and fast depreciation, especially for rehabilitation projects. These benefits became available through the efforts of the late Senator Robert Kennedy in 1969, enacted a year after the Senator's assassination. Still, about 1.5 million apartments or homes were built using public housing, Section 235 and Section 236 between 1968 and 1972. This compares well to the 90,000 per year built through Low Income Housing Tax Credits between 1987 and 2016.

In the early seventies various acts provided assistance for new communities, relocation funds, veterans housing legislation, and disaster relief.

Unfortunately, there were defaults in the early seventies that plagued many buildings and homes financed with the Section 235 and 236 programs. As Alexander Von Hoffman wrote in a 2015 paper for Harvard's Joint Center for Urban Studies, "the public-private housing programs created in the 1960s and 1970s were highly productive but many of the housing projects, buffeted by bad underwriting, weak management, and economic hard times, deteriorated badly."

One problem was that insufficient attention was given to management. Some developers had a special penchant for disaster: they calculated their management budgets by first estimating rental income and then subtracting debt service and taxes. The remainder would be the management budget. The result was that either maintenance was neglected or the owners decided not to pay debt service.

Another problem was that tenants and buyers were not eligible unless their incomes were under 80 per cent of area median. However, if management budgets had been adequate, few applicants would have qualified.

All these problems could have been fixed by amending the Housing Act of 1968 and the pertinent regulations. Instead, HUD Secretary James Lynn decided that the programs had to be studied. The "study" and President Nixon's housing moratorium are the subjects of the next chapter.

Sources for this chapter:

1) <u>HDR Handbook of Housing and Development Law</u>, 2011-12 and following, Barry G. Jacobs, published by West.

2) <u>A History of Housing in New York City</u>, Richard Plunz, Columbia University Press page1.

3) <u>How the Other Half Lives</u>, Jacob Riis, Seven Treasures Publications

4) Affordable Housing in New York, Edited by Nicholas Dagen Bloom and Matthew Gordon Lasner, Princeton University Press, 2016

5) <u>Slums and Housing</u>, James Ford, Harvard University Press, 1936, pages 5 and 251

6) The best review of early federal programs was written by a panel of experts summoned by HUD. Five study teams, each with over twenty members were involved, plus significant support staff. The title is "Housing in the Seventies, a Report of the National Housing Policy Review, HUD-0000968." It is dated November, 1974. I refer to it extensively for the history in this chapter and in the next chapter that describes the HUD Moratorium. The opposition by private realtors is well documented in 1934 newsletter provided by the National Association of Real Estate Brokers.

7) The Beautiful Beginnings, the Failure to Learn by Elizabeth Wood, published by the National Center for Housing Management

8) <u>Politics, Planning and the Public Interest</u>, Martin Meyerson and Edward C. Banfield, 1955, Free Press. This book provides a great history of public housing in Chicago.

9) <u>There Are no Children Here</u>, by Alexander Kotlowitz, Random Houses, 1992, describes the very sad state of a public housing project in Chicago.

10) <u>Robert Clifton Weaver and the American City</u>, Wendell E. Pritchett, University of Chicago Press, 2008

11) NY Times, April 16, 1973

12) Alexander von Hoffman, "Goal: A history of housing policy in the United states from the early 19th century to the present," 2015.

CHAPTER 3

The HUD Moratorium

FOR MOST OF MY adult life, if I complained about work, my father would tell me "if you have no problems, you have no business." Problems of all kinds abound in the world of affordable housing. The political problems became quite serious in the early 1970's. HUD Secretary George Romney (father of current Senator Mitt Romney) "resigned" after President Richard Nixon was elected for a second term, and James Lynn took over as Secretary. Romney had been an automotive CEO, as well as an active promoter of civil rights, perhaps a little too active to suit President Nixon and his top advisors. Romney had been defeated as a presidential candidate in the primary that Nixon won. Surprisingly, in his first administration Nixon asked Romney to become the Secretary of the Department of Housing and Urban Development.

Suddenly in late November 1972, HUD Secretary Romney announced with a high sense of drama that there would be no new commitments for housing developments financed or subsidized by the Department of Housing and Urban Development. Then he was replaced in February, 1973, by James Lynn, who had been Undersecretary at the Department of Commerce. President Richard Nixon ordered the housing moratorium to begin on January 5, 1973 and then reiterated the news about the moratorium in his 1973 State of the Union address to Congress. There would be no new projects financed under Section 235, Section 236, Rent Supplements, public housing or college housing.

Housing professionals and advocates were shocked beyond credulity. House and Senate Committees held hearings about housing subsidies intermittently during 1973. Many members of Congress were very angry about the cutoffs. Even when a federal judge ruled against the moratorium, it remained in effect pending appeal. The appeal was successful, alas. The Democratic majority of the Joint Economic Subcommittee on Priorities and Economy in Government blamed the problems on poor HUD management, not on the programs per se. Mayors, housing groups and civic organizations, including the National Association of Home Builders, the Urban League and the League of Women Voters were vehement about the negative effects of the moratorium. (CQ Almanac, On line Edition, 1973).

In New York City, housing administrator Albert Walsh and New York City Housing Authority chairman Joseph Christian called a meeting. Housing developers, nonprofit sponsors, lenders, builders, consultants, lawyers and state officials were invited. I was there with Clara Fox, Executive Director of the four-year-old nonprofit, Settlement Housing Fund. At first I was a consultant, but soon I went to work at Settlement Housing Fund full time. At my subtle urging, Clara stood up and eloquently protested the moratorium, calling for a new committee to demand that Congress "do something." This was early in 1973. Clara became the founding co-chair of the New York Coalition to Save Housing, which would morph into the New York Housing Conference in 1976.

At that time New York City's housing agencies had a long pipeline of sites that were ready for the development of affordable housing. Some were designated for new public housing, others for programs initiated as part of President Lyndon Johnson's Great Society programs, mainly the Section 236 interest rate subsidy program. Included were sites for senior citizens as well as sites for middle-income families, some of which would be partially assisted to include low-income tenants who needed deeper federal subsidies. City housing officials would meet regularly with local HUD officials to determine the priority of various sites.

The announcement of the moratorium threw everyone into despair. Clara and I quickly got the New York Coalition to Save Housing (now New York Housing Conference) into gear. I became the Staff Director. Nancy LeBlanc, Executive Director of Mobilization for Youth, became Clara's co-chair. Nancy, an attorney, was well known as a radical housing advocate who also had a practical side to her activism. Members of the Coalition board included state and local housing officials, bankers, developers, nonprofit executives, neighborhood leaders, lawyers, consultants— the entire housing industry. Although many of the members disagreed with each other on all sorts of issues, they were all horrified by the moratorium and were determined to take action. We made sure, for example, that the rent control advocates would not sit next to the head of the landlords' organization. They glared at each other, but worked together, setting the tone for decades of future advocacy.

So, what was the moratorium all about? Secretaries Romney and Lynn had claimed that programs would be suspended to allow a thorough "study" by housing experts. We were skeptical, thinking it was one of Nixon's dirty tricks. It turned out to be quite a study.

It's amazing now to read HUD Secretary James Lynn's 280-page report about "Housing in the Seventies," published in 1974. The report, cited in the last chapter, gives an excellent history of all federal laws, regulations and policies that affected housing. Five separate task forces were listed and a total of 164 participants who worked on various aspects of research and production. The report was not overly critical.

True, there were many problems that plagued affordable housing. In New York City there had been earlier problems with scandals involving the City's Rehabilitation Loan Program. Many of the state and locally financed middle-income projects suffered because of financing and some unfortunate political decisions. The developers, with the blessing of government, kept rolling over construction loans without ever locking in permanent financing. Then when long-term interest rates started to climb, the rents would not support the costs. It was also politically impossible to evict tenants who did not pay rent. The developers paid for utilities and operations instead of paying debt service, but the government did not foreclose. Foreclosure was inconceivable politically when John Lindsay was Mayor and Nelson Rockefeller was the New York State Governor.

Governor Nelson Rockefeller created the New York State Urban Development Corporation, which had vast powers to override local laws. The chief executive, Edward Logue, achieved record production numbers. Sometimes, he authorized state-financed developments before securing the federal Section 236 subsidies needed to reach moderate income families. That process worked well, allowing rapid development, until the moratorium. Economic disarray resulted almost immediately. The Corporation had financed construction with "moral obligation bonds," not guaranteed by the state. Previously there had been no instances of default. That was all about to change. For the first time investors in state and municipal bonds lost their entire investments. The Urban Development Corporation fired one third of its staff, the entire project development division. (Housing & Development Reporter, March 10, 1975). The moratorium caused the default. This would be one of the causes of New York's fiscal crisis in the seventies.

There were many problems throughout the country as well. The press focused on scandals, seldom writing about success stories. A book entitled HUD Scandals by a former HUD attorney, Irving Welfeld, chronicled the history of "howling headlines and silent fiascos" over the decades. He certainly did not dwell on housing victories. The critical report "Housing in the Seventies" by Secretary Lynn predicted that 20 per cent of Section 236 projects could be expected to fail within 10 years (page 94).

However, the fact that 80 percent were expected to succeed meant that things did not seem so terrible to many advocates.

Conrad Egan, an experienced housing expert, remembers the moratorium well. He began his career as a community organizer in Detroit. He was a follower of the late Saul Alinsky. When the Model Cities Program started in the Johnson Administration, Highland Park, a city within the Detroit boundaries, was designated as a Model City. Conrad became intrigued with the program and went to work for HUD. Model Cities was an ambitious program that coupled housing with educational programs and community activities. The program was phased down and ended during the Nixon years. Conrad was at HUD from 1969 to 1986, and then again in the nineties during the Clinton Administration.

From 1972 to 1979 Conrad was in the San Francisco Regional Office, starting out in the Phoenix Area Office and then going to San Francisco. His work included stints in production, planning and evaluation and in multifamily asset management. He was in San Francisco in 1973 when President Nixon announced the HUD moratorium, calling for a halt to all multifamily and single-family subsidized housing. He remembered that "long, long" report by Lynn, outlining the history of federal housing programs and a host of recent problems.

Charles (Chuck) Edson, a lawyer and a housing expert's expert was aghast when the moratorium was announced. He had worked for the federal government in several capacities. He was active in the antipoverty program at the Office of Economic Opportunity's legal services division. There was a sense of excitement there. Everyone worked till all hours of the night, devising new programs to address poverty. Then he went to work at HUD in the counsel's office. HUD was more of an "old line" agency, with federal housing insurance dominating the activity. It was strictly "nine-to-five." Still, when Chuck was there from 1968 to 1970, productivity in subsidized housing was at a high. He left and started a new law firm, Lane and Edson, that would specialize in affordable housing law, including advising about the intricate aspects of the tax benefits to investors and developers. And then came the moratorium. He and his associates thought that would be the end of the firm. It was as though the Sherman Antitrust Act had been rescinded just when a law firm became an exclusive expert in antitrust defense." In spite of the moratorium, the firm prospered and became Nixon and Peabody. During the late seventies and eighties, Edson would organize all-day seminars, with housing experts explaining programmatic details. Cocktail receptions would follow the seminars. HUD officials and Congressional staff members would come to the receptions, which became great meeting places for housing professionals, even during the moratorium.

Most housing professionals hated the moratorium. However, there were actual problems with the Section 235 program for moderate-income home owners and the 236 program for multifamily rental buildings. These were interest rate subsidy programs, bringing effective rates down to one per cent. Interest subsidy programs had smaller budget impacts than prior loan programs, which used the entire loan amounts when calculating the project budgets. However, there were problems with Section 236 because income limits were too low and operating budgets were underestimated.

The Section 235 Program for home ownership was experiencing defaults for many reasons. In Detroit, the appraisers (known as "Windshield Willies" because of drive-by appraisals) inflated sloppy appraisals, resulting in puffed up mortgages for inferior products. Many buyers were unqualified, and defaults mounted. In addition, in Detroit, residents of the suburbs (especially Warren) objected to the program, which would help minorities become home-owners. As mentioned above and cited by Conrad Egan, Nixon White House staff members wanted to get rid of Secretary George Romney, who had hoped that Section 235 would help to integrate the suburbs. Romney had been a long-time promoter of civil rights. It was rumored that Haldeman and Erlichman thought that Romney was a liability. James Lynn, who was relatively uncontroversial, focused on financial problems.

Richard C. Gentry, (Rick) now President and CEO of the San Diego Housing Commission, worked for many years at the Department of Housing and Urban Development (HUD), starting early in his career. As a young student, he had wanted to be a minister, and then thought he would work in the world of academia. But he decided that he preferred to be "doing something" and took advantage of an offer to become an intern at HUD in 1972.

As an intern in Chicago, he learned about all the details of housing programs. Although most people find development to be exciting, Rick was fortunate to have ended up specializing in management, an essential aspect of housing that does not get enough attention.

Near the end of 1972, he began working in the Greensboro, North Carolina regional HUD office. In fact, he was the last person hired before President Nixon put a halt to operations. Most of the staff in Greensboro and many in the Washington office were secret Nixon haters. The HUD staff in North Carolina learned that HUD Secretary George Romney, backed by President Nixon, was about to call for a "moratorium" on all housing programs. The Greensboro staff was suspicious about the "so-called plan" to study the programs for a year and then recommend appropriate changes. In the meantime, everything would stop. The staff worried that even projects that were in advanced planning probably would never happen. Luckily, the staff in Greensboro got advanced wind of the plans for the moratorium and quickly swung into action. They worked around the clock, even over the Christmas holidays in 1972 to accelerate processing. The goal was that all the projects would get to a quick construction start. And, in fact, not a single project was lost. The central HUD office in Washington conducted an investigation. Luckily, no one got fired.

The New York Coalition to Save Housing sent several busloads of protesters to Washington, meeting with Senator Jacob Javits on the steps of the Capital. I made a number of trips and met with HUD officials to assure that several projects that were just about ready to start would be spared. HUD issued regulations that permitted projects with firm commitments to go ahead. In addition, because former Secretary Romney and remaining Assistant Secretary Harold Finger, were proponents of manufactured housing construction, developments with "prefab" were allowed to proceed. These were called "exceptions" to the moratorium.

In hindsight, many professionals recall that quite a lot got done in spite of the moratorium. This was certainly the case in New York City.

In February 1974, HUD Secretary Lynn projected that the federal budget for fiscal 1975 would include funds amounting to $5.1 billion (almost $36 billion in 2021 dollars) for subsidized units. The document estimated that 300,000 units would receive funding commitments. That did not include 124,000 units in the

HUD pipeline for suspended programs, or 82,000 units of "bona fide new commitments" under these programs.

Interestingly, one program was not slated for the axe of the moratorium. This was the Section 23 Leased Housing Program, which had been enacted in 1965 and permitted housing authorities to lease units in private developments. In some cities the housing authorities would issue bonds backed by Section 23 lease commitments. The HUD budget for fiscal 1975 projected 300,000 units to be leased under Section 23, including 225,000 units of new construction and 75,000 units in existing housing. (Housing and Development Reporter, February 6, 1974). The home builders and others were proponents of Section 23, which had a reasonably good track record.

The resemblance of Section 23 to Section 8 now seems especially dramatic, as will be described in the next chapter.

CHAPTER 4

The Housing and Community Development Act Of 1974

WHEN THE NEW YORK housing community was not busy protesting the moratorium, some of us headed to Washington to obtain "exceptions" to the moratorium so that our projects could go ahead. I became somewhat friendly with two assistant HUD secretaries after successfully obtaining exceptions for several New York projects.

In early 1974, Secretary James Lynn and the various assistant secretaries began to hold briefing sessions about a proposed new housing act. This would be the Housing and Community Development Act of 1974. I was invited to one of the first sessions.

I learned that seven federal grant programs would be eliminated and replaced with block grants to localities. Urban Renewal, various planning grants, water and sewer grants and others would no longer exist. Revenue sharing programs had been popular with mayors and governors. Cities could use the block grants for any program that would benefit low and moderate-income residents. The good news was that funds could be used to address regional issues. However, I had concerns that a single source of funding would be more vulnerable to cutbacks than individual programs, each with its own advocacy group. In 2019 the Trump Administration has proposed very deep cuts. Luckily, Congress did not approve the cuts.

At the same briefing, Secretary Lynn outlined the new housing program, a proposed amendment to Section 8 of the Housing Act of 1937, the Act that originally established public housing. Section 8 would be flexible, adjusting to local needs.

Fair Market Rents would be published for different sized apartments in all the metropolitan areas across the country. Section 8 subsidies would cover the difference between the rent needed for operating and financial costs and what tenants could afford to pay for rent with 25 per cent of adjusted income. Allowable operating and finance costs could not result in rents that would exceed 110 per cent of Fair Market Rents, with very few exceptions. There would be specific Fair Market Rents for existing housing, and for new construction and substantial rehabilitation. For new construction, there would be specific rent levels for low-rise buildings and for high-rise elevator buildings. I asked whether the rent levels would be realistic. Previous programs had income and rent limits that were too low to cover costs, even with subsidies, and it was hard to develop feasible projects. I was assured that the Fair Market Rents would be realistic. The rents for existing housing would be based on a survey of recent moves, adjusted if needed to reflect specific markets. The rents for new construction and substantial rehabilitation would be based on cost indices. It all sounded pretty reasonable to me. Plus, the new budget was more than twice as high as the budget in 1972. All good.

REACTIONS:

When I returned to New York, I burst into Clara Fox's office. Clara was my boss at Settlement Housing Fund and chaired the New York Housing Conference. You will never believe it, I told her. "The new Nixon housing program is great." She glared at me and shouted, "Get out of my office."

Her reaction was easy to understand. Skepticism was warranted, and most housing officials could not believe that a workable program would ever be enacted with the blessing of the Nixon Administration. People joked, saying Section 8 was the code name for mentally ill people in the armed forces. Very few people trusted

Secretary Lynn. I was one of the believers. A few other advocates and lawyers were also supportive. Gradually the skeptics were persuaded, and although shocked, many of us worked together so that the actual statutory language was technically correct, and the programs would become effective.

THE ACT:

In writing this chapter, I decided to reread the statute, public law 93-383, the Housing and Community Development Act of 1974, which was signed into law by President Ford on August 22, 1974. Crazy as it sounds, the statute was an exhilarating read.

It began as follows: "Congress...declares that the future of its citizens depends on the establishment and maintenance of viable urban communities as social, economic and political entities that require systematic and sustained action by Federal, State and local governments...to improve the living environment of low and moderate income families..."

I especially liked the words "maintenance" and "sustained."

Then the law went on to state that its primary objective was "to provide decent housing and a suitable living environment and expanded economic opportunities principally for persons of low and moderate income." Other goals included "deconcentration of housing opportunities for persons of lower income and the revitalization of deteriorated areas to attract persons of higher income."

It was refreshing to read the aspiration of "annual assistance, maximum certainty and minimal delay."

Other provisions in Title I provided for guarantees for property acquisition loans as well as requiring prevailing wages (Davis Bacon) in all projects with more than eight apartments. Complying with Davis Bacon wage requirements, work rules and paperwork has often been onerous for developers and localities that want to use federal funds to provide as many housing units as possible.

Title II was all about housing. First came the "Declaration of Policy," which was "to remedy unsanitary housing conditions and the acute shortage of decent, safe and sanitary housing conditions of families of low income."

Next were provisions concerning the development and rent levels of public housing, Local authorities could set income limits. The statute allowed public housing authorities to rent up to 50 per cent of the units using the new program, (Section 8). Also included was a section that allowed authorities to sell units to the tenants, and another establishing a set-aside for Native Americans.

Then, importantly, the new Section 8 Program was launched as an amendment to the Housing Act of 1937. One of the purposes of the new act was to "promote economically mixed housing." And remember, this was 1974. Section 8 allowed the HUD Secretary through local agencies to enter into assistance contracts "that shall establish maximum monthly rent (including utilities) that cannot exceed 110 percent of Fair Market Rents, which would be published in the Federal Register at least annually" in different localities across the country. Under special circumstances, the HUD Secretary could allow rents of 120 per cent of Fair Market Rent. In New York there were almost always special circumstances.

In Section 8 (c) tenant rent requirements were spelled out. Tenants would pay between 15 and 25 per cent of income for rent. The statute read as follows: "The amount of the monthly assistance payment with respect to any dwelling unit, in the case of a large very low-income family, or a family with exceptional medical or other expenses, as determined by the Secretary, shall be the difference between fifteen percentum of one twelfth of the annual income of the family occupying the dwelling unit and the maximum monthly rent which the contract provides that the owner is to receive for the unit. In the case of other families, the Secretary shall establish the amount of the assistance, not less than the difference between 15 percentum nor more than 25 percentum of the family's income and the maximum rent, taking into consideration the number of minor children and the extent of medical or other unusual expenses incurred by the family." Income would be reviewed annually and every two years for the elderly.

Since this is not the time to be modest, the ratio of 15 per cent was my idea. More about that later.

Housing owners were very pleased when they learned that they would be subsidized for up to 60 days after a family vacates a unit, allowing time to prepare the apartment for the new tenant.

Up to 100 per cent of the units could be subsidized, although the Secretary could provide a preference for buildings in which only 20 per cent of the units are assisted. This provision was in deference to HUD. The contract could provide funds reserved for increased operating costs in later years. Thirty per cent of the units would be allocated to very low-income families whose incomes do not exceed 50 per cent of area median. The term "lower" income family meant "those whose incomes do not exceed "80 percentum of median."

One of my favorite provisions allowed the HUD Secretary to "establish income ceilings higher or lower than 80 percentum of the median for the area on the basis of his (or her) findings that such variations are necessary because of prevailing levels of construction costs, unusually high or low family incomes or other factors." When the Secretary had to approve something, it meant going to Washington, rather than working just with HUD's area or regional office. This provision was very useful for obtaining income integration and for dealing with special projects such as Manhattan Plaza, which will be the subject of another chapter. Section 8 had many flexible aspects, important in adjusting to regional characteristics.

Tenant selection was to "be the sole function of the owner." The owner could be a "private person or entity, including a cooperative or a public housing agency." Contractual terms would be up to fifteen years for existing housing, twenty years for new or substantially rehabilitated housing. For state or locally financed housing, the term could be up to 40 years. There was a stipulation that contracts could be "pledged or offered as security for any loan or obligation." Housing for the elderly financed with Section 202 loans could be assisted with Section 8. Financing terms had to be approved by HUD. The Section 202 clause was supported by the intensive and impressive lobbying efforts by AARP, the American Association for Retired Persons.

Local governments were allowed to submit a "housing assistance plan." If the plan was approved by HUD, the locality could object to "inconsistent projects."

As I kept reading the statute, I found clauses that call for HUD to "promote use of energy saving techniques." This was a reaction to the fuel cost crises that began in 1973. A few years later President Carter would be jokingly criticized for keeping the White House temperature at 68 degrees or below.

This Act authorized Section 223 to permit refinancing of federal, state or local mortgages. This provision helped during the City's fiscal crisis of 1976 and is still used today.

I was surprised to see the establishment of a new fellowship program, providing grants for graduate level training of planners and urban specialists in public or private universities.

There were Sections that called for phasing out older programs. Some programs, like the Experimental Housing Allowance Program would be expanded before the phase out.

It made me humble to realize that in 1974, the federal government was giving out grants to explore solar energy, and that the Act authorized federal flood insurance. If only these programs could have continued and been expanded.

The final pages of the Act dealt with a hodgepodge of items, including the elimination of previous programs. There was also a paragraph that deleted income limits for continued occupancy in public housing. One clause allowed grants for local counseling programs, and that would become important to future Secretary Carla A. Hills.

THE HOUSE DEBATE:

After reading the statute, just for nostalgia, I decided to read the Congressional Record of June 20, 1974. This was the date that the House of Representatives debated and voted to pass the 1974 Act. I had been working closely with then Congressman Edward I. Koch to support Section 8. However, I had been concerned that the rent-to-income ratios for federal housing programs, then 25 per cent, were much too high. At that time, most higher income households in the United States paid less than 15 per cent of income for housing costs. New York State housing programs required tenants to pay one sixth of their incomes for housing. I was hoping that for Section 8, Congress could reduce the ratios so that tenants would pay no more than 15 per cent of income for rent. Families would then have some funds left to pay for other essential items. No one at the time could have imagined that tenants would, starting in 1983, would pay 30 per cent of income for rent.

I decided to see if I could find Robert Weiner who, as Congressman Edward Koch's legislative assistant in 1974, had worked closely with me on the 15 per cent amendment. With the help of another former Koch staff member, Ronay Menshel, (later Deputy Mayor, head of Phipps Houses, member of the Board of the N.Y. Federal Reserve and on and on) I located Bob, who now heads a publicity firm that places op ed articles in newspapers throughout the United states. He had a distinguished career as staff to several members of Congress, Senators, committees and in the Clinton White House. He remains refreshingly concerned and articulate about the need to eradicate poverty. He was Congressman Koch's chief of legislation. I was amazed that he still believes that the current rent burden of at least 30 per cent of income for housing is excessive. He has placed several articles on the subject, including an article he wrote with the late Mayor Koch in the year before the Mayor's death. It was most exciting to meet with him partly because I had not seen him since 1974.

We reminisced about the successful debate concerning the "15 per cent" amendment. I had invited my children, then ages 8 and 11, to fly to Washington to watch the debate, but they were more interested in a "hop-on, hop-off" bus tour of Washington. They did enjoy a visit to Congressman Ed Koch's office.

Congressman Edward I.
Koch and Robert Weiner in the seventies

In 1974, Bob Weiner and I had sat in the balcony of the House of Representatives at the Capitol, watching the debate. Reading the Congressional record brought back all sorts of memories. The session was chaired by Congressman Wright Patman of Texas. He was the Chairman of the House Committee on Banking and Currency. Early in the debate he yielded to Congressman Koch, who said the members of the House Committee "have done a splendid job." He then said, "I will be offering what I consider to be a reasonable amendment... Housing is the number one need for poor people in this country."

Then Congresswoman Bella Abzug had the floor. She was famous as an advocate for women's rights and was very much to the left. She was far from quiet and could certainly turn a phrase. She spoke about the 1.5 per cent vacancy rate for rental housing in New York City. She trashed the Nixon Administration's housing moratorium and claimed that the new proposed program was "a hollow shell of a housing program." She bemoaned the loss of categorical grants including Model Cities, Section 235 home ownership subsidies, public housing and Section 312 rehabilitation grants. She mentioned the waiting list of 150,000 applicants in New York City for public housing. Congresswoman Abzug thought that the income limit of 80 per cent of median was too low; she preferred 90 or 100 per cent. At the same time she thought the protection for very low income tenants should be at 30 per cent, as opposed to 50 per cent of median income. She believed that public housing was the only way to reach tenants earning $5,000 a year or less. Nevertheless, she offered her "reluctant support" for the new programs.

However, Bob and I were enthusiastic about the new housing program. I was quite surprised when Bob said that he regretted that Congressman Koch (Ed) was too soft-spoken. He should be more aggressive in his speeches, "like Bella." Of course, when Congressman Koch became Mayor Koch, no one would ever think of him as soft-spoken. Quite the opposite.

As Mayor he had to implement quite a few budget cuts after the fiscal crisis of the seventies. Still, in his last term he became the best housing Mayor ever.

MORE DEBATE:

The debate went on. Congressman Robert Steele, a Republican from Connecticut, made a special plea for housing for the elderly and handicapped. Congressman Thomas (Lud) Ashley, a Democrat from Ohio and chair of the Housing Subcommittee, claimed that after 20 years in Congress, he was pleased to praise HUD's recent cooperation with the subcommittee. He was still bitter about the moratorium and reminded his colleagues that President Johnson's 1968 Act had a goal of 600,000 housing units a year. Congressman Ralph Metcalfe of Illinois "rose in opposition." Like Bella Abzug, he preferred the categorical programs.

Congressman Jonathan Bingham lamented that Section 8 was an "untested program." But, he said that his friend, Congressman Koch, was going to introduce an amendment that "must be adopted."

Congressman Michael Harrington of Massachusetts sadly noted that the program was "far short from fulfilling" the 1949 goal of a decent home for every American, the goal of the 1974 Act, He claimed that "418,000 units in one year" was "a drop in the bucket of real need." Although true, the proponents of today's federal programs are happy with 90,000 units annually through the Low Income Tax Credit Program. What's more, other sources of funds—usually from states or localities—must be added to make the complicated Tax Credit Program work.

The next speaker was Congressman Edward I. Koch. It was the moment that Bob Weiner and I had been waiting for. He introduced the amendment that I (representing the New York Housing Conference) had proposed. Instead of paying 25 per cent of adjusted income for rent, families would pay 15 to 20 per cent of adjusted income. Nine members of Congress co-sponsored the amendment.

Congressman Thomas (Lud) Ashley, the chair of the housing subcommittee, asked whether Congressman Koch would consider a substitute amendment. Ashley suggested that flexibility was important. He preferred rents to range between 15 and 25 per cent of income. He thought that large families and the very lowest income families should pay 15 per cent of income. However, he thought that some of the higher income families could afford to pay 25 per cent of income. Ironically, I worried that the higher income families would have trouble paying 25 per cent, because the actual number would be quite high. I thought it would be difficult for families with two wage earners who had to pay taxes not fund or child care.

Congressman Koch replied to Congressman Ashley, "In the interest of compromise, I would urge support of the amendment offered by the gentleman from Ohio."

Congressman Ashley responded, "There has been nobody, but nobody, on the committee or off, who has been a greater champion for the interest of the very poor people in this country…than the gentleman from New York, Mr. Koch."

The amendment was agreed to without objection. Congressman Ashley walked across the room to shake Congressman Koch's hand. This was the first amendment that Congressman Koch had ever offered.

After the successful amendment, the House took up a new version of a program to house the elderly, Section 202. The American Association of Retired Persons, AARP, representing 6.5 million members, was out in full force to lend support. Through AARP's leadership, B'nai B'rith, the American Baptist Service Corporation, the United Presbyterian Church, the National Council on Aging and the National Tenants Organization added their support. I watched in awe of AARP's clout as the program was supported by all members of the House.

Left to right: Charles (Chuck) Warren, head of legislation for Senator Javits, Cathy Catterson, Chuck's assistant, and the late Senator Jacob K. Javits

Then it was time for the vote on the bill, as amended. There were 351 "ayes," 25 "noes," and one member who voted "present." The next step was the conference with the Senate. The conferees accepted the House amendment regarding rents that would range between 15 and 25 per cent of adjusted income. On August 13, 1974, the Senate passed the Housing and Community Development Act of 1974 unanimously. Senator Jacob Javits, and the head of his legislative staff, Chuck Warren, were essential supporters. On August 15, the House voted 377 to 21 in favor of the Act. As mentioned above it was signed into law by President Ford on August 22, 1974, 13 days after President Nixon's resignation.

This was a pretty gorgeous law.

Sincere appreciation to Professor Roderick Hills, William T. Comfort Professor Law, NYU Law School for giving me access to the NYU Law School Library.

CHAPTER 5

Section 8 Success Launch

AFTER SECTION 8 WAS signed into law on August 22, 1974, the regulations had to be written. The Act was supposed to become effective in January, 1975. How do I describe my excitement, amidst the skepticism that prevailed in the world of affordable housing at the end of 1974?? I'll try.

Many advocates complained that things were taking much too long. The draft regulations for new construction and separate regulations for substantial rehabilitation were published for comment in November, 1974. Fast forward to 2021, and it seems that the process was remarkably fast. The regulations for existing housing came two months later.

Still, affordable housing developers tended to forecast problems, especially because of the negative HUD moratorium and the impeachment and resignation of President Nixon. Barry Zigas, a young reporter at the time, wrote an article in the Housing & Development Reporter in January, 1975, entitled "Leased Housing—Stumbling to the Starting Gate." After a number of interviews, he found "little enthusiasm, and plenty of doubts—even outright gloom—regarding the leasing program."

The regulations seemed pretty reasonable to some of us. HUD agreed to process mortgage insurance concurrently with housing assistance payments contracts for most Section 8 new projects.

That was much better than going through two sets of reviews. Eligible tenants had to earn less than 80 per cent of the median for local metropolitan areas. However, for each project at least 30 per cent of the units had to be rented to "very low income" tenants whose incomes did not exceed 50 per cent of area median. The legislation only required that 30 per cent of all units nationally had to be rented to very low-income tenants. Still, HUD officials thought that the "project-by-project" method was more "efficient and effective".

The regulations spelled out tenant rent contributions. Large very low-income families (below 50% of median) with six or more minors would pay 15 per cent of income for rent. Large low-income families (80% of median) with 8 minors would also pay 15 per cent, as would families with "exceptional medical or other expenses" such as child care. This would all change dramatically during the Reagan Administration.

Other families would pay 25 per cent of income for rent. However, they could deduct $300 per child as well as medical and other expenses when calculating income.

GOALS AND PROBLEMS:

Secretary Carla A. Hills, newly appointed by President Ford, could not promise the Senate to commit to reserving more than 40,000 units for fiscal 1975. At the same time, she claimed at the same Senate hearing that she could foresee over 400,000 reservations in the following year. Senator Willian Proxmire, the powerful Chair of the Appropriations Committee, was skeptical. "Yeah, sure," was the reactions of the housing community. However, Secretary Hills gained credibility when HUD actually approved reservations for 95,694 units by the end of June. (Housing Development Reporter, (HDR) July 14, page 165).

In early 1975 there were stumbling blocks that made it difficult for state and local finance agencies to provide financing for Section 8 developments. The overall economy was suffering a downfall. Interest rates were becoming much higher. Some agencies had issued bond anticipation notes, and would need to charge higher rates to replace these notes with permanent financing. Builders complained that their projects would not be feasible with higher rates. In the meantime, there were possibilities of default on the notes. This problem was especially prevalent in Massachusetts. (HDR, 8/25. Page 300).

Secretary Hills had to put out quite a few fires. The House Ways and Means Committee was considering legislation that would eliminate several tax benefits. It was important to assure that the benefits would remain for subsidized housing. Otherwise developers had little incentive to participate. (HDR, September 22, page 382)

At first Secretary Hills concentrated on reorganizing HUD to improve communications and maximize productivity. "She shook up the place, there's no question about it" according to an anonymous FHA official (HDR, 7/28/75, page 229). She initiated monthly communication with HUD's 47 Area Officers so that she could learn about problems and work on solutions. This was considered an "early warning" system and a method of quelling potential scandals. There was a heavy load of response. Secretary Hills would assign a member of the staff to respond to each Area Director within a week. There were complaints about funding notifications, for example, and Secretary Hills responded as necessary.

New guidelines required HUD to establish processing deadlines of 30 to 60 days to review development proposals in the Area Offices and reserve funds. Regulations had to be tweaked every so often to allow staff to meet these deadlines. Not easy. (HDR, 9/25/75, page 346).

At first, Secretary Hills was less popular with Congress than had been her predecessor, James Lynn. She did not tend to slap backs. Pretty soon all that would change. She would gain the respect of Congress and the industry because she got results.

The Tandem Plan helped the financing process. A first banks were wary of Section 8. In the middle 1970's mortgage defaults had reached an all-time high. Most banks were willing to make construction loans for up to 24 months, but were nervous about permanent financing.

The Tandem Plan allowed the Government National Mortgage Association, GNMA, to provide long term financing for FHA insured mortgages, up to forty years, as a "take out" for the construction loans provided by banks. The interest rate was 7.5 per cent, well below market at the time. The Tandem Plan was especially important in the mid-seventies when, as noted, long term interest rates were sky high, threatening the ability to achieve rents that were less than the HUD Fair Market Rents for new construction. Even though the Fair Market Rents were increased for many areas, including New York City, in the March 31, 1975 Federal Register, the Tandem Plan was still important as a development incentive. Moreover, GNMA set a goal of site appraisals and market analysis (SAMA) within 30 days, as opposed to the typical 60 day review.

In early February, 1976, major construction unions agreed to eliminate several restrictive practices in order to reduce the cost of rehabilitation. Secretary Hills was pleased. There were estimates that in high cost areas, rehabilitation costs could be reduced by 25%. (HDR. February 9, 1976, p.856).

As described in chapter three, there had been defaults in the early seventies in FHA financed multifamily developments and in Section 236 subsidized units. In 1976, HUD decided that 110,000 Section 8 units would be reserved for troubled FHA insured developments, an early bail out.

Congress members and advocates were still complaining. Congressman Henry Reuss called the program a "tremendous, resounding dud." (HDR 3/8/76 p.945). The National Housing Conference called for 1.2 million government assisted housing units, to catch up to the goal of 600,000 units a year, the goal of the Housing Act of 1968. Secretary Hills stayed with the Ford Administration goal of 500,000 assisted units, including 400,000 Section 8 units. (p.950)

EXISITING HOUSING:

In April 7, 1975, the final regulations For Existing Housing were published, clarifying the rent calculations and allowing the program to become feasible, soon to take off. And by mid-April reports were coming in from localities that the program was starting to produce results. (HDR, April 19, page 1113).

In New York City, Settlement Housing Fund's Executive Director, Clara Fox, sent an invitation to several landlord groups to meet with the staff and with Harold Sole, who was in charge of the Section 8 Existing Housing Program at the New York City Housing Authority. We were able to explain the program. At that time there were quite a few vacancies, especially in apartment buildings in lower income communities. The Section 8 housing assistance payments were appealing to the owners who attended. They were especially pleased that the regulations delegated tenant selection to the building owners. Settlement Housing Fund obtained foundation grants from the Rockefeller Brothers Fund and the New York Community Trust to establish a computerized data bank of apartments available for prospective tenants. We would then hold briefing sessions for the prospective tenants. We would sometimes provide bus tours for tenants to new neighborhoods where there were vacancies and standard apartments. The goal was for the Housing Authority to take over the databank, which happened a few years later.

NEW CONSTRUCTION AND REHABILITATION:

At the same time in New York, the Area Office was becoming more and more efficient in expediting reviews for new construction and substantial rehabilitation.

John Kelly, who has been one of New York City's most prominent housing attorneys, was a young lawyer at HUD Area Office from the spring of 1975 until the end of 1978. He remembers that at first there was an internal struggle about how to set the maximum rents for new construction and substantial rehabilitation. Initially, rents were supposed to be "comparable" to rents prevailing in various neighborhoods. However, the rents in most poor neighborhoods were extremely low in New York City because of the combination of abandonment and rent controls. It would have been impossible to cover the cost of debt service and operations with the very low rents that prevailed in most low-income neighborhoods and in many middle-income areas. Approved Section 8 Rents for new buildings eventually were set to reflect actual construction costs and operating budgets, rather than the "market." Secretary Hills wrote a letter to Congressman Les Aucoin to change the former policy on day before she left office. This made all the difference. (HDR,1/24/77)

When Carla Hills replaced James Lynn as HUD Secretary, in March, 1975, the final regulations still had not been published. She took care of that problem expeditiously. The regulations were changed nationally to allow rents to reflect local construction costs, enabling developments to proceed. The new regulations also included a clause that I had helped to draft for the New York Housing Conference. A special allocation was provided for recently completed housing. This will be discussed in a later chapter about Manhattan Plaza, a large development on West 42 Street.

At the end of 1975, Secretary Hills had to battle OMB for enough Section 8 money to achieve HUD's objectives. She took a chance and released a plan to Congress and the White House with 54 goals that she hoped to achieve. There were six categories of goals, including one entitled "PROVIDE DECENT HOUSING." There were 29 s subheadings, ranging from processing 95 per cent of all applications for conditional commitments for single family housing within 5 days to providing 400,000 reservations for Section 8. After a difficult battle with OMB, she was able to secure budget authority for 125,000 units of Section 8 for new construction for fiscal 1976. The Housing Authorization Act of 1976 was approved in August, 1976. Single nonelederly individuals became eligible for Section 8. This would become important in New York and in the eighties when homelessness began to emerge.

Secretary Hills still had to contend with opposition in Congress. There were efforts to divert Section 8 funds to public housing and other programs. Secretary Hills agreed to a set aside for public housing, but it was limited in the appropriations bill. Regulations and guidelines were adjusted, as required by local experience. And indeed, Secretary Hills achieved her goal. Over 400,000 reservations were sent out for fiscal 1976, an all-time high. Unfortunately, (for housing, not for her) President Ford appointed Carla Hills as U.S. Trade Representative. HUD never reached that record of reservations again. Maybe next year—as Brooklyn Dodger fans used to suggest after a losing season.

Reservations were one thing. Actual construction was another.

In the late seventies Section 8 took off at a pace that few had anticipated. For state or locally financed projects, HUD did not require duplication of reviews for design standards, environmental effects and other issues. Whenever possible, reviews were delegated to state or local agencies. HUD was trying to do everything possible to assure the success of Section 8 in getting commitments out to developers.

Charles (Chuck) Edson, an excellent lawyer and founder of John Kelly's firm, had a great sense of humor. He presided over the Leased Housing Association, formerly the Section 23 Leased Housing Association, referring to an earlier program. Chuck organized seminars, explaining how Section 8 would work. I attended many of them along with my first boss, Roger Schafer, who was a lawyer and consultant and the expert who had taught me all about the economics and regulations regarding affordable housing. We liked Chuck's teaching techniques. In the late seventies we began our own dinner seminars. After I started working as the Associate Director of Settlement Housing Fund, I became even more of a Section 8 aficionado. At one point I was invited by the New School to chair an all-day seminar about the program. I included City officials, HUD representatives, The Housing Authority, landlord and tenants' representatives. It was a rare occasion for me—standing room only. (mainly because of the other panelists).

PRODUCTIVITY

Much more important, the program took off locally. Developing housing with federal assistance had been a painfully slow process. In the late 1960's and early 1970's, whenever I would inquire about a HUD commitment or a review, I was told that it was "in typing." The reviews took forever and a day. But, when Alan Wiener became Area Manager of the New York HUD Area office, everything changed dramatically. The staff was even coming to work on Saturdays in order to fast track the review and commitment of Section 8 developments.

Alan headed the New York Area Office from 1978 until 1981. He now heads the municipal finance division of Wells Fargo. I was lucky to be able to interview him as I was writing this chapter. He worked for New York's housing agency when John Lindsay was Mayor. He went over to City Hall after Abraham Beame became Mayor of New York. When I spoke to him In 2020 he was very busy, working from home on housing finance during the pandemic.

When Patricia Harris became HUD Secretary for President Carter, she recruited Alan Wiener to head the New York Area Office. He totally transformed operations. Alan admired Secretary Harris and had an excellent working relationship with her. Lawrence Simons, who had been a successful Staten Island builder, became Assistant Secretary and FHA Commissioner. Alan managed to talk to Simons every day, thereby avoiding potential snafus in Washington. He was able to produce ten to twelve thousand housing units a year, using project-based Section 8 for new construction and substantial rehabilitation. I asked him how much had been done in prior years. He had a beautiful one-word answer: "bubkis."

I continued the discussion, asking him how he managed to transform the staff. He said they were good people, and they wanted to achieve positive outcomes. And he motivated them. He would "yell occasionally,"—(probably an understatement). He also "had their backs," which was inevitably true.

Alan Wiener was careful to choose qualified sponsors and developers, but he did not play favorites. And having excellent relationships with New York City and Washington officials was certainly helpful. He also worked well with officials in Westchester and Long Island. Alan was the first, perhaps only, HUD field office employee to receive a Presidential Award. He recalled, pleasantly reminiscing, that Secretary Patricia Harris came to New York to attend his retirement party. He has continued in the private sector to play a most important role in all aspects of housing, especially finance. I was very pleased that he still believes that Section 8 was an excellent, workable program. He agreed with me that it could be amended to assist everyone in need of affordable housing.

HUD continued to conduct briefings for the housing community about Section 8, encouraging qualified organizations to apply. Even after Alan Wiener left his post at HUD, federal officials reached out to local officials to set priorities so that coordinated approaches could be facilitated. Developers worked hard to convince New York City officials that their proposals should be on the "high priority" list.

John Kelly agrees that Alan Wiener energized the HUD Area Office. He encouraged teamwork.

John's immediate boss, the Area General Counsel, was Ben Skurnick. Before Alan Wiener became Area Director, Skurnick had been able to find all sorts of reasons to delay or even to reject projects. He was known as "No-no Ben." Somehow Alan miraculously transformed him into the world's most energetic lawyer, who was able to push legal approvals on to a fast track system. John Kelly developed an excellent working relationship with Ben in this positive mode.

FRIENDSET:

Settlement Housing Fund was able to develop several projects that benefited from early reservations and the efficient review process at the area office of HUD. One project was a co-venture with the Friendship Club of Maimonides Hospital, a group of senior citizens advised by Dr. Sidney Saul, a geriatric psychiatrist. The Club leaders were Pauline Affronti and Frieda Laufgraben, two women who had spectacular senses of humor. Their dream was to build housing for the elderly with a geriatric senior health center on the first floor. The City officials suggested a site in Coney Island to be one of the first Section 8 new construction projects. They did not know right away about the health center. The Friendship Club members liked the Coney Island site. We called the project Friendset. (Friendship Club and Settlement Housing Fund) The architects designed a simple building, 20 floors with 259 apartments. We included 240 one-bedroom units and 19 two-bedroom apartments, intended for individuals who needed live-in assistance. The design called for a 7,000 square foot health center on the first floor. Coney Island Hospital agreed to sponsor and staff the facility

This was the first project for which I prepared all the documents by myself except for the architectural drawings. Included were a financial plan, a cost estimate, a management plan, a project description, background material regarding Settlement Housing Fund, the Friendship Club, the contractor, Reuben Glick, the mortgagee, Huntoon Paige, the management company, and letters of support from local politicians and community organizations. We included a geriatric social worker on the operating staff, which was very controversial. There were six copies of thirty documents required. The proposal was due the Tuesday after Memorial Day in 1977. On the Friday before Memorial Day weekend. I brought all the documents home plus six large green loose-leaf books and a hole puncher. I did not get dressed the entire weekend, which was spent reviewing each document, collating and filling the loose-leaf books. I brought the thirty booklets to the HUD Area Office just in time to meet the deadline.

HUD approved the plan. Next came the local review process and the State review of the health center.

Because it was very difficult for HUD to approve nonresidential uses for FHA insured projects, I was worried that the health center would be eliminated. I projected a very low rental rate for the center—$3 a square foot. I was sure someone would object. Instead it sailed through. We did have to redesign, because city officials were worried about a shadow on the low-rise buildings across the street, (which were demolished a few years later). One of the City Planning Commissioners wanted to make sure the chain link fence around the perimeter had very small holes so that juvenile delinquents could not easily climb over to vandalize the building. The building began construction in late 1977 and remains 100 per cent occupied today. Settlement Housing Fund did not stay in as long term owner, but visited the development for many years to check up on everything.

Years later I was invited a number of times by a professor at the Columbia School of Planning to talk about my experiences. I would talk about all the issues in developing Friendset, ending by saying that it was the easiest development of my career. I went back to look at the building in 2012, after Hurricane Sandy. Very little damage was done. The health center was active with many clients in the waiting room. There was a plaque, honoring Settlement Housing Fund, listing me as consultant. There was a beautiful photo of the late Sidney Saul. Settlement Housing Fund attempted to join another organization to buy the project for $32 million. The total development cost in 1977 had been less than $10 million. Other groups outbid us, paying over $40 million. The project remains 100 per cent assisted by Section 8.

This project and so many other new and existing buildings benefited from this early launch of Section 8.

CHAPTER 6

Impoundment and the Budget

LATE IN 2019 IMPOUNDMENT suddenly became part of the news. A lawyer and another staff member of the U.S. Office of Management and Budget (OMB) even resigned from their jobs, in protest because of unlawful impoundment. They claimed that President Trump had violated the Budget and Anti-impoundment Act of 1974 by withholding funds that had been appropriated by Congress for the defense of Ukraine. As the Trump impeachment trial began, the Government Accounting Office (GAO) staff decided that Trump had indeed violated the 1974 Act. "Faithful execution of the law does not permit the President to substitute his own policy priorities for those that Congress had enacted into law," the GAO wrote. Everything old became new again.

A few months earlier, Elizabeth (Liz) Holtzman, a former member of Congress, had been on television, also talking about impoundment. She said that former President Nixon had also impounded funds at the beginning of the Watergate scandal. I knew Liz from my college days, and she was an important member of Congress in the 1970's, when I was protesting the HUD moratorium described in a previous chapter. I called Liz to discuss the impoundment issues of 1973 and 2019. She had been on the House Judiciary Committee that was in charge of the Watergate investigation.

Although President Nixon was not impeached for impounding funds, impoundment contributed to the context of impeachment and added to the public's overall distrust, recalled Congress member Holtzman. Nixon impounded funds for housing construction, for measures to combat water pollution, for open space, highway construction, water and sewer grants, agriculture and education. There were 30 lawsuits against federal agencies, 25 of which were successful.

As I read about impoundment, I learned that Nixon was not the first President who had impounded funds. Far from it. The first was Thomas Jefferson in 1803, when he impounded funds that had been appropriated by Congress for gunboats. Because peace had been achieved in Mississippi, the boats were no longer needed. Congress did not object. However, later when Jefferson refused to pay the salaries of certain government officials, "Congress threatened and the President retreated." The fact that a program was no longer needed was the only reason for impoundment until the administration of Franklin D. Roosevelt. President Roosevelt did not spend appropriated funds for several programs, but Congress did not object because of the depression and World War II.

The Omnibus Appropriations Act of 1951 contained an attachment that allowed establishing "reserves for contingencies" or savings through "efficiencies or other developments..." Presidents Truman, Eisenhower, Kennedy and Johnson did not spend all appropriated funds, mostly because the purpose had to do with military operations, which were no longer needed.

President Nixon's impoundments were different. Previous Presidents notified Congress before impounding funds. Nixon did not. He impounded funds simply because he did not like specific programs. He justified his actions at a press conference on January, 31,1973, claiming that he had a constitutional right to impound funds when "Congress overspends." Congress disagreed.

Localities were negatively affected. Professor Irving Goffman, an economist at the University of Florida estimated that impoundment prevented the creation of 100,000 jobs. (N.Y. Times, October 7, 1973).

Still, it is sometimes difficult to distinguish between unlawful impoundment and instances when all appropriated funds are not spent. There have been times when HUD rushed to spend research funds. "Use it or lose it" became a frequent slogan. Legislation could be required to re-appropriate funds that remained unspent, but this was a lengthy, uncertain process.

In 1990 Congress authorized a President to use a "line item veto," to avoid using funds for specific programs. This certainly sounds like impoundment. The Supreme Court ruled that the act was unconstitutional.

The case of Pennsylvania vs. Lynn was one of the few cases regarding impoundment that the Nixon/Ford Administrations eventually won. (Ironically, the victory came three weeks before the new Section 8 program was signed into law). The Pennsylvania lawsuit dealt with the HUD moratorium, discussed in a previous chapter. The District Court had ruled against HUD, mainly because Congress had appropriated funds for specific programs, and HUD withheld funds for new commitments of these funds. HUD appealed, and the Court of Appeals overturned the District Court's decision. The decision was interesting. It contained detailed descriptions of three housing programs that had been suspended.

It was pointed out that funds were suspended to determine whether the programs were effective. "When the Secretary has evidence sufficient to convince him that particular housing programs have come into conflict with the overall housing policy or the program goals set by Congress," and when an administrative fix is impossible, there is justification to suspend funding new projects. HUD's action was not taken to save money or because of the President's disapproval of Congressional goals. Impoundment was constitutional if done for a good reason.

I spoke to Robert Elliot, who was HUD's General Counsel in the seventies. He spoke of many instances when there was pressure to use funds before Congressional expiration deadlines. He said that impoundment of funds appropriated by Congress was unconstitutional when "planned and intentional" in defiance of appropriation acts.

The Congressional Budget and Impoundment Control Act of 1974 was supposed to fix all that.

In 1972, Congress formed a new committee, "held hearing after hearing and produced a 4,600-page record of testimony and reports." The new Budget Act was passed on July 12, 1974, just before President Nixon's resignation. (Kevin Kosar, Politico, 10/2015). Before the Act, the process had been quite vague. The president would send a budget to Congress. Then Congress would pass appropriation acts accordingly. The appropriations could not exceed the amounts that had been authorized by the relevant congressional committees.

The one exception was for public housing, which was not subject to the appropriations process. Annual contributions contacts between the federal governments and local authorities supported bonds issued by the authorities. The contracts were subject to the full faith and credit of the United States. After 1969, operating subsidies were added so that residents would pay no more than 25 per cent of income for rent. All that would change after 1974.

The Congressional Budget and Impoundment Control Act established budget committees in the Senate and the House. A new Congressional Budget Office would be formed to provide information to the committees by October 1 of each year, based on the proposal submitted by the President. The change of dates gave Congress enough time to respond to the President's budget.

The Act mandated using up-to-date computer technology. The Act also set October 1 as the beginning of the federal fiscal year. Other measures set time parameters for submitting budget proposals. The President and the Committees were required to include five-year projections in their budget authority proposals. Today most budget items are projected over ten years. That exercise makes each item seem huge, especially when not dividing by ten.

Budget resolutions needed to be set before appropriations could be provided. A deadline of May 15 was set, giving time for consideration before the new fiscal year, which would begin on October 1.

When the Budget Act was first being reviewed in 1974, I was far from pleased. Most people were happy with the anti-impoundment aspects of the law. To me, the new budget process just seemed like a waste of time. We already had a slew of committees to deal with. First there are subcommittees in the House and Senate that authorize maximum funds for specific programs. Then the subcommittee recommendations go to full committees. If the House and Senate versions differ with one another, a final decision by a conference committee is required. The President has to sign the conference bill. Then the same thing happens again when funds are considered by the appropriations committees. Often the appropriations committees provide less than the authorized amounts. The process seemed to take forever. To add another layer of review by the new budget committees would delay the availability of housing funds even more. That seemed unconscionable. Enough already.

The result turned out to be even more problematic than I had anticipated. Before the Budget Act, the deficit was calculated by subtracting outlays for various departments from tax revenue. However, starting in 1976, Section 8 contracts were calculated in the budget by adding up all the obligations for the entire term of a housing assistance contract. I remember that Budget Director (OMB), former HUD Secretary James Lynn said that the HUD budget went from one of the smallest to one of the largest in one year. This seemed like a distortion. It made HUD programs an easy target for a cut.

I spoke to Anthony Freedman, who had been the staff director for the Budget Committee from 1974 to 1976. He explained that because Section 8 contracts ranged from 15 to 40 years, the Committee had to provide budget authority based on the entire contractual amount, especially when considering expenses backed by the full faith and credit of the federal government. If budget authority was calculated by estimating outlays, there was a danger that HUD would be forced into default. If future budget committees did not provide adequate authority, the trouble could be serious.

Tony was at HUD from 1978 until 1981. He had the responsibility of testifying before the congressional budget committees. At first glance, the budget authority per housing unit looked huge. Supposing there was a 30-year Section 8 contract for 100 apartments, and the annual cost per unit was $5,000. The budget authority per apartment would be $150,000.—much more than the price of a single family home in some of the legislators' districts. It was hard for Congress members to understand the calculations of budget authority.

It was especially hard for housing advocates to swallow. Leon Weiner, a developer who was president of the National Housing Conference said it was like calculating the cost of a battle ship by including the cost of 30 years of repairs, cleaning, fuel and the salaries of the sailors. Others said it was like saying the cost of a house included 30 years of interest and amortization payments on the mortgage. Yes, I know that cleaning battle ships and paying interest on individual mortgages were not backed by the full faith and credit of the United States. But still.

One evening during those years I met a staff member of OMB at a reception. He was in charge of the housing budget. He was the only person I knew who was pleased with the method of preparing the Section 8 budget. He knew that budget authority for the term of a contract would make the program seem more expensive than other programs. He did not like the Section 8 program because it relied on private developers. He preferred public housing.

Eventually Assistant Secretary Lawrence Simon shortened the contractual term to one year. The contracts allowed annual renewals. Secretary Simon assumed that the contracts would keep being renewed.

Although funds have been drastically reduced over the years, the commitments to renew Section 8 contracts have been kept. The contracts are always subject to annual appropriations. Even today, it feels very risky. Still, so far, so good. Some of us still worry. In chapter 11, I include an interview with a tenant who is very worried about the possibility that that funds could be eliminated and that she would lose her home. The problem is worrisome.

The calculations of budget authority were and remain obscure. It is somewhat easier to look at the number of housing units produced. Anne Lindgren, who was a Special Assistant at HUD during the Carter Administration once told me that there were many ways to calculate production. One could count commitments, construction starts, or occupancy or a combination. She was only half joking. However, there is no getting around the fact that Secretary Carla Hills was able to use the budget allocation to produce 417,000 subsidized rental housing units in 1977. Even during the moratorium, exceptions resulted in 274,000 units in calendar year 1973. (CQ Almanac, 1973). The last budget in the Carter administration called for about 280,000 units. Half would be for new construction and substantial rehabilitation. The other half would be for existing housing. In 1983, during the Reagan Administration, the number dipped to 2630 units. That was the year that HUD eliminated the Section 8 Program for New Construction and Substantial Rehabilitation.

All in all, the method for calculating the housing budget is opaque. I can understand the logical reasons for including the entire amount of a contract in budget authority. But the numbers seem very scary. I can also understand the reason to change the rules to provide one-year renewable Section 8 contracts. Perhaps the budget for housing could have had two columns, one for the contractual obligations and another for anticipated annual outlays. The outlays would be the actual numbers used by Congress.

Although funds have been drastically reduced over the years, the commitments to renew have been kept. The contracts are always subject to annual appropriations.

All in all, I like the "anti-impoundment" part of the law, but I believe that the rules for budget authority need to be clarified and simplified. I remain a devout housing advocate, as well as a budget skeptic.

CHAPTER 7

Carla A. Hills

IN THE FALL OF 1974 there were rumors that James Lynn would leave HUD for another position in the Ford Administration. As it turned out, he did leave and became the Director of the Office of Management and Budget (OMB) in 1975.

On a Saturday morning Carla A. Hills was about to leave with her husband and two children for a long anticipated trip to the Washington Zoo. Then the phone rang. It was President Ford. He wanted to see her right away. Ergo, no the trip to the zoo.

Instead, she went to the White House immediately. The President said, "Carla, I want you to be my HUD Secretary."

"But President Ford," she replied, "I'm not an urbanologist".

"I don't care," said the President. "I need a manager."

There had been many rumors before the announcement. To the surprise of everyone in Congress and in the industry, President Ford did in fact nominate Carla A. Hills as HUD Secretary. At the time she was an Assistant Attorney General in the Justice Department and had very little housing experience. She had been in charge of the Civil Division at the Justice Department and did in fact work with HUD attorneys on various lawsuits and legal issues. But that was it.

The American Institute of Architects, The National Rehabilitation Association and the National Housing Conference asked the White House to withdraw her nomination. The National Association of Home Builders expressed doubts, calling the nomination a "deep disappointment." Senator William Proxmire said that the country needs "a Secretary of Housing who can build houses." There were many more colorful objections. In her testimony, she did not pretend to have housing experience, but she seemed to care about housing issues, was very knowledgeable about the new programs and devoted to high productivity. Senator Proxmire was the only Senator who voted against her nomination, bemoaning her "total ignorance" of housing programs.

Eventually, after he retired from the Senate, he sent her the following note:

"Dear Carla:

I voted against you. I'm sorry.

Bill."

In my opinion, Carla A. Hills was the best HUD Secretary in any administration since HUD began in 1965. Although I admired Robert Weaver and Shaun Donovan, Carla Hills not only shares my passion for Section 8, but her ability to get results is breath taking.

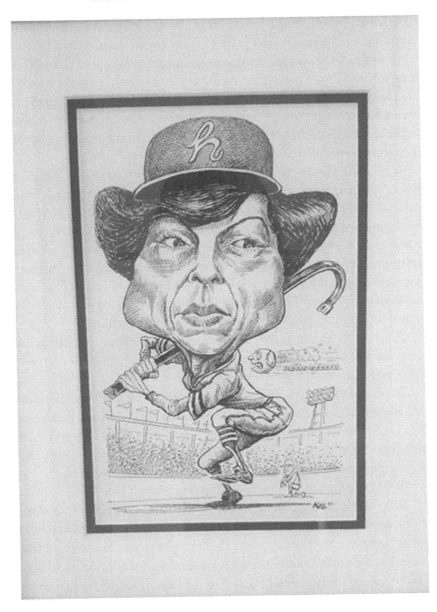

I met with Ambassador Hills in July, 2019. (I refer to her as both "Ambassador" and "Secretary," depending on the circumstances). After leaving HUD she was U.S. Trade Representative from1989 to 1993. She is currently president of a consulting firm that "advises companies and organizations on matters of international trade and investment, diplomacy and politics." My secret opinion is that her work with all the disparate organizations in the world of affordable housing must have been great training for her work on global issues.

Her company's office is beautiful, located in the Georgetown area of Washington, D.C. We met in the large conference room, and she described her efforts as HUD Secretary. To me, her most important comment was, "I believe in Section 8."

Carla Hills began her tenure at HUD in March, 1975. Congress held Authorization and Budget hearings beginning in June. She was asked, "How many units can you get out in this fiscal year?" Her answer was "none." After all, there were no regulations. Writing them was a process that she had just begun. Gathering all her courage, she promised to create approximately 500,000 apartments the next year, including at least 400,000 Section 8 units. This was an enormous commitment. Even during the Johnson years, the maximum annual production was under 200,000 units.

As it turned out, the regulations were quite workable, as described in the previous chapter. And indeed, in fiscal 1977, there were reservations for over 490,000 units.

How did she do it? She told me that she would meet with all the Regional Administrators and Area Managers and ask them one by one, "How many units can you get out?" She would have regular meetings to keep track of their progress and to resolve issues and any impediments to production. It seemed to have worked.

490,000 plus units. How does one argue with that?

Secretary Hills gives a lot of credit to the leadership of President Ford, a president whom she very much admired. President Ford held weekly meetings with all the cabinet secretaries. Secretary Hills would sometimes take issue with James Lynn, Director of OMB. (Housing advocates would call the agency "TOMB," because of OMB's constant advocacy for funding cutbacks). Secretary Hills talked about an example. She asked for an authorization of $10 million for educational programs to help tenants get ready before moving to Section 8 buildings. Jim Lynn did not want to approve the funds, but Secretary Hills was able to convince President Ford to approve the funding allocation anyway. In fact, President Ford was very supportive of funds for housing programs. "Leadership matters," Secretary Hills told me.

I mentioned that I also had been an admirer of President Ford, but could not vote for him because Senator Robert Dole was his running mate. Senator Dole had opposed funds for housing. Ambassador Hills nodded, but then affirmed that President Ford was a great leader. She said that he knew that when he pardoned Richard Nixon after Watergate, he would not be reelected. But, he told her, that was the only way to convince Nixon to resign. Ms. Hills said that President Carter was "a nice man" but very weak. President Carter and President Ford became close friends after their presidencies. Ambassador Hills mentioned that Carter, after leaving office, cured worm diseases in Africa. She was quite respectful of that accomplishment.

The backdrop of this period of time was extremely challenging. Double digit inflation, high unemployment, the high cost of fuel, the Vietnam War, May Day riots, the aftermath of Nixon's resignation—turbulence all around. Achieving consensus about housing production was an even more amazing accomplishment given the atmosphere.

Carla Hills does not believe that "Washington knows best." She admires the Community Development Block Grant Program, established along with Section 8 in the Housing and Community Development Act of 1974. "The conditions in Phoenix are not the same as in Newark," she told me. In Newark, there was very little open space. In Phoenix there were no available buildings to rehabilitate. The block grant program replaced 14 individual categorical grants, including such items as rat eradication, street lighting, park and sewers. Local governments, she believes, are better attuned to and know about the severity of local problems. The block grant program allowed flexibility. Similarly, Section 8 allowed localities decide how much money should be used for new construction or rehabilitation or for available units in existing buildings. The fact that fair market rents varied according to regions was another illustration of acknowledging regional variations.

"One size does not fit all."

Ambassador Hills mentioned that she had been a close friend of the late Cushing Dolbeare, an advocate who established the Low Income Housing Coalition. I was quite surprised. Dolbeare was passionate about serving the poorest of the poor. She also wanted to divert the home-owners' tax deduction to support low income housing, a very unpopular goal at the time. She won a MacArthur Award and donated the funds ($500,000) to support her organization. Although I admired her and liked her, I thought it was equally important to assist all income groups that could not afford decent, safe housing. I kept telling her about the importance of mixed-income housing. We supported each other but did not always agree. Still, Cushing Dolbeare was articulate and dynamic. I was pleased that Ambassador Hills had been her friend.

Ambassador Hills gave me two large, very heavy loose leaf books that contained 49 speeches about housing which she had given in 1975 and 1976. The groups whom she addressed were varied— ranging from the NAACP to the American Bankers' Association to the YWCA of New York.

An article on page 18 of the New York Times described how George Romney, HUD Secretary for President Nixon, had advocated "withholding federal money from communities that blocked housing for lower-income and minority families." President Nixon "halted the idea". Secretary Hills, with the full backing of President Ford, "unhalted it." She defunded communities several times when it was possible to prove violation of fair housing acts. President Ford, a graduate of an integrated high school, supported desegregation. Carla Hills emphasized withholding funds from cities that violate fair housing laws in a speech at a conference sponsored by the National Association of Colored People, (NAACP) on June 2, 1975. She also spoke passionately at the Fair Housing Conference on April 29, 1975, about HUD's plan "to reduce or cut revenue sharing" to combat Fair Housing Act violations.

At a HUD Awards ceremony on October 29, 1975, she listed all the complaints she heard as HUD Secretary. She said "they all had a common denominator: MONEY." She kept returning to that theme. I personally believe that housing can succeed over the long term only if there is enough money to build a building properly as well as an adequate budget for management and maintenance. She also decried "waste," alluding to the fact that 50,000 buildings had been abandoned in New York City.

In another speech commemorating HUD's 10th anniversary, she mentioned that 82 per cent of the net population growth between 1970 and 1973 consisted of single individuals or married couples without children. This is a trend that has continued over the decades. She described a new program to encourage middle income home ownership, using the Government National Mortgage Association (GNMA) to purchase mortgages from banks and then reducing the interest rates on the loans. Her goal was 500,000 home ownership units during the next two fiscal years, which she achieved. Her claim was that 500,000 construction jobs would result. All one needs, Secretary Hills claimed, was "energy, ingenuity, and horse sense."

She told the Republican Women's Club that the issues "all boil down to 16 million Americans living in slum-level housing, and it's HUD'S job to do something about it."

Again, she cited the need for money. She claimed that the "Blame does not totally lie with racists or ineffective officials. Rather, it is apparent that economic and social problems have grown far faster that our capacity to forge new solutions."

Secretary Hills was smart politically. She stressed the importance of "state and local decision making," when addressing the National Governors" Conference. When speaking at a meeting of the NAACP, she spoke about lowering the amount of rent for large families to 15 per cent of income. And, the "rental subsidy is open ended," she underscored. HUD's site selection criteria would hopefully encourage neighborhood integration, and Section 8 for existing housing allowed tenants to choose where they wanted to live.

High productivity was a constant theme, whether addressing Jessie Jackson's organization or the American Bar Association. The fact that 16 million American families are "housing poor" was simply unacceptable. In a speech before the National Rehabilitation Association, Secretary Hills again claimed that the job cannot be done without money.

In another speech before the National League of Cities, she mentioned her concern about the Budget and Impoundment Act, which would take effect in 1977. She thought one answer was revenue sharing, an idea that had to be popular with localities. She also spoke about the plans for GNMA to purchase 500,000 mortgages over the next two years for middle income families.

Secretary Hills suggested at a meeting of the National Association of Home Builders that the members should "go out and get a trumpet" to promote the homeownership plan and make it work.

At the Republican National Conference in February, 1976, Secretary Hills promised 55 residential demonstration projects that would utilize solar energy for heating and cooling. How's that for an idea that is relevant and innovative today?

At the same meeting, she emphasized the flexibility of Section 8 with the programmatic ability to adjust to local needs. The locality was best suited to determine whether the subsidies should be used for existing housing, rehabilitation of buildings or new construction. At a meeting later that month before the Business Council, she noted that HUD reserved 490,000 Section 8 units during the fiscal year.

I recalled meeting with Secretary Hills, urging that several New York projects receive expedited approvals from HUD in order to maintain favorable construction agreements. I was accompanied by a colleague, Sandra Thomas, who was representing the Upper West Side of Manhattan. Sandra would bristle if anyone dared to call her a liberal. "I'm a radical," she would shout. We had previously met with the New York State commissioner, Lee Goodwin, who worked for Governor Nelson Rockefeller and his successor, Governor Malcolm Wilson. As we left the meeting with Secretary Hills, Sandra said to me, "I like Republican women better than Democrat men." I think she was serious.

I left her office in 2019 just as impressed as Sandra and I had been back in the seventies. Maybe even more so. Her current work involves advising a variety of American and international clients about international trade opportunities and issues. She has an impressive array of partners and associates, and her office is beautiful. I asked for copies of two photos. One was with Presidents Ford and Carter, after the trade agreement with Mexico and Canada was signed (NAFTA). She was the key proponent of the plan. The other was a cartoon, showing her with a large cigar in her mouth. She laughed and explained that the cartoon presumably indicated that she was "tough." She said she would send me the photos when she got back from China. In addition to her professional activities, she serves on many corporate and nonprofit boards. For example, she is President Emeritus of the Council on Foreign Relations and is Chair of the National Committee on U.S.-China Relations.

I wish she were still the Secretary of HUD. If only we had Carla Hills as a housing leader, perhaps we could achieve the goal of the National Housing Act of 1949 :

"a decent home in a suitable environment for every
American family."

CHAPTER 8

Manhattan Plaza and Program Flexibility

SECTION 8 CONTRACTS WERE used to assure the development and financial viability of housing developments throughout the country. As described in the previous chapter, HUD Secretary Carla Hills demonstrated how effective the program was in developing desperately needed affordable housing. In addition to stimulating maximum housing productivity, the statute and regulations allowed flexibility and consideration to the needs of localities and neighborhoods. Manhattan Plaza is an excellent case study.

Manhattan Plaza is a very large New York City development, home to many movie stars. A documentary film, "Miracle on 42 Street," describes how actors who were poor in the seventies were so grateful to live in Manhattan Plaza before they became famous. They're still grateful. Angela Lansbury, Tennessee Williams, Estelle Parsons are among the stars who were well known before moving there. Alicia Keyes grew up in the development and practiced on the piano in the community space. Larry David met Kenny Kramer, who lived across the hall, and that was the beginning of Seinfeld. The film tells a lot about what happened, but did not tell about all the geeky stuff and controversy that took place in order to create the financing and subsidies that made everything work. There were people who did not speak to me for decades because of my role in this development.

WEST 42 STREET IN THE SEVENTIES AND THE BIRTH OF MANHATTAN PLAZA

Manhattan Plaza is a high-rise development on West 42 Street with 1,689 apartments. It was completed in 1976, a time when West 42 Street was a high crime area, notorious for porn shops, prostitutes, drug dealers and x rated movies. The developer, Dick Ravitch, and the contractor, HRH, had impeccable reputations. Dick, now a well known civic leader, bought the site from another developer at a very reasonable price. He was able to convince City Hall to use its Article XII bond program to finance the construction of middle-income housing. Permanent financing would come from the City's Mitchell Lama Program, named for two state legislators and used by Robert Moses and others to finance middle-income housing. Hopefully the result would be the beginning of a revival of the neighborhood. The views of the Hudson River would be spectacular. Ravitch was even able to persuade the housing officials that an Olympic-sized swimming pool and tennis courts should be included in the complex to attract middle-income tenants to the neighborhood. The architect was the late David Todd, a former landmarks commissioner who had a great eye for design as well as pragmatic ability to get through the city's approval process. Irving Fisher, the construction guru at Ravitch's company, HRH, oversaw construction.

The national and the local economies began to suffer while Manhattan Plaza was under construction. Adjusted to 2017 dollars, the price of crude oil would have been $22.35 in 1968 and $55.51 in 1975. (Inflation Data.com). Interest rates nationally went from 6.81 per cent in 1968 to 9.43 per cent in 1975, and kept on a course of escalation.

Rents needed to soar to cover costs; they climbed to levels over twice the estimates made at the beginning of construction. The original projection was $85 a room, standard at the time for the Mitchell Lama Program. By 1976, the necessary rent was $179 a room. That would be $800 a room today, or $2,800 for a one-bedroom unit. In 1974 there was no way that middle income families could afford the new rents. Only tenants looking for a bargain would have been willing to move to West 42 Street in the first place. No one in any part of New York City would be willing to pay enough rent to cover the increased costs, especially not on 42nd Street. What to do?

The City Administration decided to use the newly available federal Section 8 Program. But, after the plans for subsidies were announced all hell broke loose. The League of Theater Owners, the Schoenfeld Organization and the Broadway Association sued the City. Poor people would ruin the environment, they argued. Other theater owners joined in. Community residents claimed that the local residents needed housing even if they were not performing artists. Advocates from other neighborhoods protested, claiming that Section 8 was desperately needed in low-income residential areas of the City, especially the Bronx. Congressman Herman Badillo, a member of the House housing subcommittee, was especially upset.

When the Section 8 program was in its initial years, I was working with the City Administration and Congress on behalf of the New York Housing Conference on comments on the initial Section 8 regulations. My colleague, John Maguire, a City official, and I had prepared our comments regarding the proposed new regulations. We asked for an allocation of funds for recently completed buildings. At that time, in the mid-seventies, there was a glut of condominiums that were not selling because of the fiscal crisis of the seventies. We were both very proud of our idea and the regulations that we drafted. And even better, HUD actually adopted our suggestions. Manhattan Plaza was a perfect fit for the new regulations. (John later became the head of the California housing finance agency, and several years later he passed away from AIDs).

Still, in New York, protests were mounting. It was hard to persuade protesters that Manhattan Plaza was one of the few "recently completed" developments eligible for the special Section 8 allocation.

SETTLEMENT HOUSING FUND TO THE RESCUE

At that time I was Associate Director of Settlement Housing Fund. Clara Fox, who founded the organization in 1969, was Executive Director, and Susan Cole was the tenant selection specialist. Roger Starr, Housing Commissioner, and Dick Ravitch called us and asked for a meeting. Ravitch had hired our organization to select tenants in another large development. Starr and Ravitch suggested a consultant contract with Settlement Housing Fund so we could recommend a strategy for selecting the tenants at Manhattan Plaza. We had a second meeting at the chambers of our Board Chairman, the New York State Supreme Court Judge Harold Baer. Starr and

Ravitch seemed in awe of the surroundings and the presence of Judge Baer, wearing his black robe. Several other board members were present.

Our board was hesitant because of all the controversy. My reaction was, "We need to have some fun. Let's do it." The board approved the contract.

The first step was for Settlement Housing Fund to form a board committee that would recommend a tenant selection process, including recommendations regarding subsidy programs. We invited other developers and management experts to suggest ideas. One of the first to be interviewed was a developer named Dan Rose, president of a prominent real estate company, Rose Associates. Dan's company developed, owned and managed luxury developments and middle income projects. He spoke and wrote elegantly, often including Latin phrases is his writings. He suggested renting the apartments at Manhattan Plaza to actors and actresses because of the development's proximity to the theater district. He was quite flamboyant in his presentation. He described how the performers could enjoy nude parties in the swimming pool—after all this was the seventies. He thought that the federal 236 program would be best suited for the development. Section 236 was not known as a program for the poor, even though the income limits were the same as Section 8 and public housing. Even after the HUD moratorium, New York had a small allocation of section 236 funding, but there were some glitches that made the program hard to use. There were also reasons that the program would not work well for performing artists.

Settlement Housing Fund's committee liked the idea of housing for performers. Coincidentally, Clara Fox, Susan Cole and I had been invited to a few meetings with a committee from Actors Equity about co-sponsoring housing for actors. We needed to figure out the income levels of performing artists. We hired David Muchnick. David was both a lawyer and a PHD. He had just left the City government, having served as housing policy director and was pleased to take the job. The opponents of Section 8 subsidies (League of theater owners, the Broadway Association and the Shubert Organization) had hired David's former boss, Al Walsh, as their lawyer. Al had been Housing Commissioner for the state and then for the City during the Lindsay Administration. We told Al about the proposal for actors' housing. Al was sure that we would be sued for discrimination.

CREATING HOUSING FOR PERFORMING ARTISTS

David got right to work. He created a questionnaire that would result in a survey of the incomes of performing artists. We met again with representatives of Actors Equity. We also met with the Screen Actors' Guild, (SAG), and representatives of other performers, including ballet dancers and even ushers. David issued a report showing that most performing artists earned very little money. In addition, even well known actors had some very bad years. Often performers incomes fluctuated wildly from year to year.

After reading David's report, the Settlement Housing Fund committee recommended that apartments be reserved for a mix of incomes, ranging from very low income to those who could afford the full Mitchell Lama rent ($179 a room). The committee decided to include everyone who worked in performing arts, ranging from well known stars to ushers.

Eureka. Section 8 would be ideally suited to subsidize Manhattan Plaza as housing for performing artists. At that time Section 8 tenants paid between 15 and 25 per cent of adjusted income for rent. (The lower rent-to-income ratio was for large families). The federal government paid the remainder of the cost of operations, debt service and taxes. The payment was made through a housing assistance payment contract between the federal government and the housing owner. The contractual term for municipally financed projects was up to 40 years. Manhattan Plaza was fortunate enough to obtain a 40-year contract.

The best reason for using Section 8 was that the program was ideal for tenants with fluctuating incomes. If a tenant's income went up, his or her share of the rent would go up accordingly. Similarly, if income went down the tenant would pay less. Incomes were certified annually.

POLITICAL AND LEGAL ISSUES

Of course, there were problems at both the local and federal levels. We wanted approval from the local community board, not an easy task. The City Planning Commission and the Board of Estimate (now the City Council) had to approve the plan. Even worse, the only single people eligible for Section 8 had to be either elderly or handicapped. That would leave many performers (young and single) out of the picture. We would need to amend the federal statute. Even though city officials included the amendment as part of its annual legislative package, changing the law became my responsibility.

We were lucky. Congressman Edward I. Koch was a member of the housing subcommittee. I had worked with him and his staff on other amendments. He came to several meetings of the New York Housing Conference when I was staff director. I also had a good relationship with the counsel to the committee. The amendment was added to the draft House housing authorization bill.

Next I approached Chuck Warren who was head of Senator Jacob Javits' legislative staff. He had written major environmental laws, as well as the War Powers Act, limiting the ability of the President to declare war without the approval of Congress. He also wrote a number of amendments that allowed federal housing programs to be effective in New York City. He agreed that Senator Javits would offer the singles' eligibility provision to the pending housing bill. He was concerned, however, about a potential problem. Carl Coan, the head of the Senate Committee staff had 13 children and thought that single people had many options and did not need Section 8. Chuck was persuasive. The Senate amendment allowed single individuals to be eligible in areas where there were few smaller apartments affordable and available. The Senate provision remained in the final version of the bill. This was not a problem because there was no doubt about the shortage of housing in New York City for everyone, including singles. Chuck Warren's photo is in Chapter Four. He is now a leading environmental lawyer as well as long-time Chairman of the Settlement Housing Fund Board.

Gaining community support was an equally daunting problem. Why the preference for actors when so many community residents needed decent, affordable housing? I asked my boss, Clara Fox, whether it was fair to favor performers. She was quite eloquent. She said that artists and performers enrich everyone's lives. In her experience, actors tend not to be prejudiced, accepting all races, religions, and they tolerated gay people. She was quite convincing, and carried the ball in the community. We all sought the approval of the local clergy, which we obtained. We met with the leaders of some of the political clubs. Still, Al Walsh, the prominent attorney who had been retained by the opponents, spoke at a large community meeting. He said he would "bet his career," that we would lose in a lawsuit. He was sure that that preferences for actors violated fair housing laws. In fact the City and the developers were sued, but not successfully. Luckily, no one took Al up on his bet.

Eventually we won over the community board by agreeing that seventy per cent of the apartments would be reserved for all members of the performing arts. The other thirty per cent would be rented to community residents, half of whom would be senior citizens who lived nearby.

Next we needed the approval of the City Planning Commission and the Board of Estimate. Well known actors became advocates, including Angela Lansbury.

Even the renowned Helen Hayes testified before the Board of the Estimate. All the members of the audience and the Board, (including Mayor Beame) stood up and applauded when she entered the hearing room. The plan was approved unanimously.

It still wasn't over. We were able to take advantage of the allocation of Section 8 for recently completed buildings. However, the locally approved plan called for a mix of incomes that would require HUD to use its power to waive the income limits for 30 per cent of the apartments. The Section 8 income limits were set at 80 per cent of median for the metropolitan area. The Secretary of HUD had the statutory authority to set limits that were higher or lower in areas with high construction costs or unusually high or low incomes. Settlement Housing Fund had been able to convince

HUD to raise income limits to 100 per cent of median for ten per cent of the units in a lower Manhattan building. For Manhattan Plaza, our plan called for 30 per cent of the units to be allocated to tenants earning up to 135 per cent of area median income. This was not an easy sell. Again, we appealed to Senator Javits and Congressman Koch. At that time Anne Lindgren, one of my closest friends, was a special assistant to the HUD Secretary, and she was persistent in her support. Eventually HUD relented.

Our plan also called for ten per cent to the units to be rented at "market" rates for the Mitchell Lama Program, with much higher income limits. HUD officials were worried that we would not be able to rent these units. After all, why would market rate tenants ever want to live on West 42 Street next door to poor people? In unusual generosity, HUD provided a Section 8 contract for 100 per cent of the apartments. Amazingly, we had no problem renting the 10 per cent market rate units. We tried to give funds back to HUD and to the City for a while, but none of the agencies knew what to do with the money. We kept the excess funds in a reserve, in case one of the government agencies asked for the funds to be returned or for emergencies. When Clara Fox retired in 1983, she was surprised to learn that she had been elected as an honorary member of Actors Equity. She moved into one of the market rate units on the thirty-first floor.

TENANT SELECTION

The next job was to select the tenants. The developers hired Rose Associates (Dan Rose's company) as managers. Stuart Shatkin was our contact. One day he came to see us to get our thoughts about hiring an Episcopal minister as the on site manager. The idea sounded a bit strange. The minister was the Rev. Rodney Kirk. He had been responsible for all the musical programs at the Cathedral of St. John the Divine. He was also the person who brought the tall ships to the New York Harbor for the celebration of the bicentennial anniversary of 1776, which had taken place in 1976, just before the plan for Manhattan Plaza was approved. We wondered what does all that has to do with housing management. Rodney won us over completely during his interview. The combination of charm, passion and attention to detail was quite dazzling, even to Clara Fox, who was initially quite skeptical. Richard Hunnings was also retained, and he was someone who understood the physical plant of buildings—even how to maintain the swimming pool. He and Rodney were a great team. Richard continued to work there until he retired in 2014.

The next job was to form a committee (known as the "policy committee") to begin advertising and letting the community know about how tenants would be selected. One issue was how to determine who would qualify as a performing artist. The job of tenant selection consultant was Susan Cole's. Susan was both a certified social worker and licensed real estate broker. In addition, she was a tenant selection expert. (I was terrible at tenant selection because I never wanted to turn anyone down).

Susan and Rodney Kirk were on the committee, as well as representatives of eight unions, including Actors Equity and Screen Actors Guild. The process included credit checks and required copies of tax returns. To qualify as a performing artists, at least fifty per cent of an applicant's income had to come from the arts. The performing artists and community residents were mixed on all floors, as were the different income bands. I remember one time that Rodney and Susan were joking and said it would be easier to require glossy photos and use them for selecting tenants. There were over 5,000 applications for the 1,689 apartments. The first tenant moved to the building in June of 1977. The policy committee is still in charge of tenant selection today.

AFTER OCCUPANCY

I remember the day of the dedication. It took place in the Ellington Room on the first floor. Not only were the usual politicians and government officials there, but to my surprise, my favorite jazz quartet provided great music. The saxophonist, Russell Procope, an early Manhattan Plaza tenant, was also a member of the Brooks

Kerr Quartet, my favorite group that performed every night at a bar on East 63 Street called Gregory's. I had been to many ceremonies for numerous dedications, but this was a favorite.

Settlement Housing Fund continued to act as tenant selection consultant, and Susan and Rodney hired the staff that would interact with tenants. One of the first programs was devoted to the elderly population at Manhattan Plaza. This was the Stay Well Center. There were also programs for children, including a summer camp and a day care program organized by the parents who resided in the building. Rodney thought that it was important for all the children in the building to learn to swim, and lessons were provided. In addition, the Junior Tennis League offered tennis lessons through a citywide program organized by a tennis aficionado, Skip Hartman. The League still operates in low-income neighborhoods throughout the city.

Suddenly in the eighties, the AIDs epidemic became especially tragic at Manhattan Plaza. Some of the tenants died from the disease. That led to a call for action by Rodney and Susan's husband, Pyser Edelsack, who was a Professor at Sophie Davis Medical School. They developed a medical clinic and therapy for those who would die or were very ill. It was operated by a newly created nonprofit organization. Many of the Manhattan Plaza residents volunteered. Everyone on the management team pitched in.

Everything seemed to be working out even better than had been expected. The buildings were immaculate. Security guards kept the buildings safe, as did the turnstiles required for entry and the mirrors. Tenants made good use of the ground floor space and the baby grand piano. The policy committee organized the use of the space.

Politicians visited and had their photos taken. Joan Mondale, wife of Vice-President Walter Mondale, visited and was very impressed, suggesting that the project be replicated in other areas. We were worried when we learned that HUD Secretary Patricia Harris was about to visit. We did not know how she would react to the swimming pool and the flamboyant gay tenants who liked to sunbathe at the pool.

Luckily, the visit went well.

MANHATTAN PLAZA OVER THE YEARS

Rodney Kirk passed away in 2001. Irv Fisher, who had been in charge of construction, became the de facto manager, sharing responsibilities with Richard Hunnings. He was meticulous and loved the project. The Stay Well Center became the Rodney Kirk Center. As the population grew older, the programs for the elderly expanded. Today the staff includes a program director, a certified social worker and two additional staff members. In addition, there are physicians and nurses retained as consultants. By 2016, 52 per cent of the residents were over 62 years old.

Most of the costs of the various program are paid from the management budget, although the residents paid a small fee. There are still programs for children even though only about 150 children live in the 1689 apartments. Skip Hartman of the Junior Tennis League, arranged for these children to have access to the school across the street from Manhattan Plaza after school hours and during summers.

In addition to the policy committee, composed of artists union representatives and managers (and Susan Cole), a small tenants association existed, sometimes in a contentious relationship with management. Marisa Redanty, who had been active in Actors Equity and the Screen Actors Guild, became the secretary of the association in 2001, and was soon elected chairperson. She continued as chair for a decade. The relationship with management improved. The tenants association became much more active. In earlier years about 6 people would attend the meetings. Attendance grew to hundreds of members when the relations with management got better.

NEW OWNERS

But a new problem was in the making. Kenny Kramer called Marisa and told her about his conversation with a reporter from the New York Times. The reporter asked for Kenny's comments about Dick Ravitch's plans to sell Manhattan Plaza to another development company, the Related Companies. The story would break the next day.

Beginning in the nineties, project-based Section 8 contracts around the country were expiring. Some of the more successful owners were converting their buildings to market-rate housing. Most of the original Section 8 advocates had not anticipated that problem. (I worried back in 1974, and people laughed at me). The original owners of Manhattan Plaza had formed a limited partnership to take advantage of tax benefits. The partners were aware that the Section 8 contract would expire in 2017. In addition, there were developers in New York who had opted out of the Mitchell Lama Program to get rid of restrictions and to take advantage of the improved market.

Dick Ravitch had invited me to have a drink with him. He asked me what I thought would happen if he converted some of his buildings to market rate housing. He said that some of his investors were putting pressure on him. I told him in no uncertain terms that there would be a revolution if that happened at Manhattan Plaza, and I would help to lead it.

In 2004, Ravitch and his partners did in fact sell Manhattan Plaza to the affordable housing branch of the Related Companies. We had always worried about what would happen when the contract expired in 2017. Hopefully Related would renew the Section 8 contract and keep the building as an affordable development. Jeffrey Brodsky, a Vice-president of Related, was assigned to oversee management.

When he met with Irv Fisher, Jeff remembered how Irv reacted. Irv walked over to Jeff and glared. He pressed his finger firmly on Jeff's nose and said, "Don't fuck up my building. Keep the building affordable. Do not cut security or social programs." That would be Irv's legacy.

The tenants received updates through postings and newsletters during the nine months of negotiations. Marisa and Mary Lou Westerfield, now Chair of the policy committee, met with the tenants, assuring them that they would not be kicked out. Tenants would stop Marisa in the lobby, and she would always provide an impromptu update. Two senior members of the Related Companies, Jeff Brodsky and Mark Carbone met with the tenant leaders. Marisa insisted that the head of the company, Stephen Ross, attend the next meeting with her and Mary Lou. She invited Council Member Christine Quinn to attend, as well as staff members from the offices of State Senator Tom Duane and Jerry Nadler, now a prominent Congressman. Marisa brought a pie from the Little Pie Company, one of the first commercial tenants at Manhattan Plaza. That set the tone. Steve Ross didn't know what to make of the meeting. He was quite impressed with the clout of the tenants' representatives.

The tenants association hired an experienced real estate attorney, Stanley Berman, to represent them. Marisa and Mary Lou acted as co-lead negotiators. At the next meeting, Marisa read a list of concerns. Twenty union representatives attended, including the AFL-CIO and the Teamsters. Related had only three representatives, sitting at the other end of the table.

This was a large meeting. The tenants, who often had better things to do than to attend a meeting, were invited. As it turned out, 600 residents showed up, in addition to the City Council member and the State Senator. Irv Fisher spoke, as did Jeff Brodsky, Negotiations went on for nine months. At another meeting at Actors Equity Council, 20 unions were represented as well as representatives from HUD and the city housing agency.

Rather than submit a written list of demands, Marisa and Mary Lou waited until Related drafted an agreement. They would mark "NO" next to specific paragraphs and send the agreement back. Round and round they went. Stanley Berman couldn't get over the final result. "Your side wrote the deal," he exclaimed. He had never seen a situation in which landlords agreed to all the requests by tenants.

THE CURRENT SCENE

The good news is that that Related has retained Manhattan Plaza as a Section 8 development and in the City Mitchell Lama Program. Capital improvements continue. Security and social programs are intact. However, the tenant population has grown older. At least 700 apartments are now occupied by tenants who are over 62 years old.

There are always problems in many aspects of owning and managing residential properties. The staff at Related is required to comply with city and federal regulations and supervision. The regulations often conflict with each other. The city Mitchell Lama Program requires waiting lists to be published. HUD requires that the lists must remain private. The city submitted paper monthly subsidy reports to HUD with hundreds of pages. Every other developer in the country used HUD's computerized program known as TRACS. City officials did not want to pay for TRACS because Manhattan Plaza was their only locally financed project with project-based Section 8.

After many years, HUD officials suddenly noticed that the incomes of some of the residents were very high, and that 10 per cent of the apartments were not occupied by Section 8 tenants, but instead by so-called market rate tenants. This was unheard of for most Section 8 projects. The original arrangement had long been forgotten. Luckily, many of us who worked on the original plan were still involved.

The indefatigable tenant leader, Marisa Redanty had a copy of the original Section 8 contract, with a memo from HUD Secretary Patricia Harris attached. The memo spelled out the reason for the alternate income limits. Jeff Brodsky argued vehemently to maintain the original income limits. I got in touch with HUD Assistant Secretary, Carol Galante, who had been the head of an excellent San Francisco nonprofit. (She is now a Professor at University of California, Berkeley). She said to me jokingly, "Oh, it's all your fault." Luckily, the HUD Secretary, Shaun Donovan, was a New Yorker who remembered Manhattan Plaza fondly. The old income limits, which allowed a broad income mix, were maintained. However, HUD officials finally demanded that the ten per cent unused Section 8 had to be given back. Instead, Related negotiated and promised to use Section 8 to finance a new Section 8 building on West 29 Street. Related was successful of fast tracking this new development.

However, HUD created another problem. There was a new policy mandating that 40 percent of Section 8 apartments would be rented to extremely low income tenants—those who earned less than 30 per cent of median income. It is hard to find active performers with extremely low incomes. The original 8 performing artists unions are still represented on the tenants selection committee. Related has maintained the 70 per cent set aside for performing artists, but everyone has to scrounge to find them because of the new income limits.

I asked Jeff Brodsky what was his most serious concern. He said that he worried about Section 8 funding. Even though Related had continued to extend its Section 8 contract, the funds depend on annual appropriations by Congress. Funds for public housing have been cut substantially. Could the same thing happen to project-based Section 8 ? The funds come from the "discretionary" segment of the federal budget. So far funds for existing contracts have been maintained, and most housing professionals believe that funding will continue. Still, Jeff and other housing owners and advocates worry. So far, so good.

Related had extended the Section 8 contract when becoming owners. Most recently, Related extended the contract a second time, for another 20 years, and committed to remain in the Mitchell Lama program for 6 years. City officials initially complained; eventually they shrugged. They were happy that Section 8 would protect the low-income residents for at least 20 more years.

The Section 8 rents were increased to reflect the market in the neighborhood, allowing Related to make a significant profit.

Mary Lou Westerfield remains an important advocate. She grew up in the Chicago suburbs and was a dance major at Butler University in Indiana. She became an active member of Actors Equity and the Screen Actors Guild. She and her husband, moved to New York in the seventies, living in a tenement on West 48 Street and 10th Avenue, "literally on the wrong side of the tracks." The bathtub was in the kitchen. She had to use a stepstool to get into the tub. Her husband was an actor and also a copywriter, "one of the mad men." Mary Lou and her husband and a few neighbors watched Manhattan Plaza during construction. "Who in the world would live there", they wondered. "It was the wild west." In 1978 Mary Lou joined the Screen Actors Guild Board and became a member of the Actors Equity Council. When she learned that 70 per cent of the apartments at Manhattan Plaza would be reserved for actors, she became interested, and became a representative on the policy committee. She has been a member ever since and is now co-chair of the tenants association.

Mary Lou and her husband started to worry about living in their grungy apartment on West 48 Street. How long would they be willing to have to climb into the bathtub? She applied to Manhattan Plaza and was placed on the waiting list. Seven years later, she received word that she and her husband were accepted and in 1984, the couple moved there.

Mary Lou talked about her neighbor, an actress who had been on Broadway in Zorba the Greek and Fiddler on the Roof. They became friends after being in the same yoga class. She is now very frail, living on social security and a small pension. "I don't know where she'd be if it weren't for Manhattan Plaza," Mary Lou told me, with a dramatic sigh.

West 42 Street is certainly a different place today. Immediately after Manhattan Plaza was constructed, a row of off-Broadway theaters was built across the street. New restaurants located nearby, replacing the porn shops. Luxury housing and fancy commercial buildings soon followed. The most serious problems are the throngs of tourists and all kinds of traffic: cars, pedestrians, clowns and strange creatures in costume.

CHAPTER 9

The Cost Conundrum

(cartoon below from New Yorker in the late eighties.)

"*Frankly, a zillion still sounds high.*"

SECTION 8 IS SOOOO expensive. Sure. Attacks on the program came from all over. They still do. But many of the criticisms about comparative costs of housing programs are not accurate. The costs of Section 8 are out there—clear to see. The costs of tax benefits and other fragmented and complex housing subsidies are not so obvious. Every investor, bank or government agency "leverages" everybody else, but the total cost varies only slightly, among different programs, especially if one assumes a similar scope of work and that the incomes of the assisted residents are roughly the same.

In New York City, where high construction costs dominate, federal rules lead to even higher costs. The Davis-Bacon Act of 1931 mandates prevailing wages and difficult compliance rules for federally funded construction and renovation of buildings with more than eight subsidized apartments. These requirements are very costly. I like to see workers get a good salary. However, some of the work rules seem excessive and add unnecessarily to costs. Federal environmental rules and design standards also result in higher costs. City programs do not always have all these rules. When comparing the cost of federal and local programs, apples and oranges is an understatement. Try apples and porcupines.

Often the cost estimates for earlier federal programs did not allow enough funds for management and maintenance expenses. From time to time there were defaults because the estimates of maintenance costs were way too low. More often, low estimates led to deferred maintenance. The same was true for some of the local programs. For Section 8 new construction and substantial rehabilitation, the management budgets were realistic and default rates were very low. Most buildings were well maintained.

In the early years of the program, for budget purposes, it was assumed that tenants would pay nothing. The tenants' share of rent (15 to 25 per cent of tenants' income) was kept in a reserve fund in Washington to take care of the cost of future rent increases. Most housing professionals thought this was a good idea. In 1979 several HUD officials suggested changing the policy so costs would not seem so high. (HDR, 2/5/1979, p.852). HUD decision makers resisted at first. Then the policy was changed the next year, even though a HUD study calculated that the reserves would cover cost increases in most cases for the length of the housing assistance payments contract. Eliminating the reserves was a questionable move.

SENATOR PROXMIRE

Senator William Proxmire, a prominent Democrat from Wisconsin was head of the subcommittee of the Appropriations Committee that was responsible for housing. He was well known for his "Golden Fleece Award" which he bestowed on what he considered unworthy uses of federal grants. He gave out the "prizes" from 1975 to 1987. One example of a Golden Fleece Award winner involved a grant of $57,800 to the Federal Aviation Administration for the "study of physical measurements of 432 stewardesses, paying special attention to the length of the buttocks." A second was an award to the National Science Foundation "to compare aggressiveness of sunfish that drank tequila as opposed to gin." No one wanted one of Proxmire's "prizes."

In the seventies, I remember that Senator Proxmire could not understand why it cost $50,000 to build a two-bedroom apartment in a high rise building in New York City. It was much cheaper in Wisconsin.

WHY IS NEW YORK SO EXPENSIVE ? AND LOOKING FOR WAYS TO CUT COSTS

The costs in New York were real, as far as I could tell. It was and remains much more expensive to build in New York and in other high cost cities than in many other areas of the country. I used to read various national cost indices ruefully when advocating for federal programs that would work in New York. There are many reasons why costs are higher in New York. Although union labor is expensive, the rates are as high in some cities where total costs are lower than in New York.

Getting materials to New York is one costly problem. High rise is more expensive than low rise. Soil conditions in New York City often need costly remediation. Rock, water and debris seem to be underground everywhere, and therefore foundations are very expensive. There are many reasons. However, Congress kept objecting to the cost of the Section 8 program nationally.

In April of 1978, Senator Proxmire and Congressman Edward Boland of Massachusetts held hearings during which they criticized the cost of Section 8 new construction projects. They suggested that public housing was cheaper and a better alternative to Section 8. Secretary Patricia Harris cited a study showing that the cost of public housing is only about $80 a year less than Section 8 housing, when considering the extra cost of operating subsidies and tax-exempt bonds. She said that public housing is "cheaper on the budget, but it's not cheaper in fact." (HDR, April 17, 1978)

Both houses of Congress continued during the summer months to complain about the cost of Section 8.

The headline in the July 24,1978 edition of "Housing and Development Reporter" read as follows: "Subcommittee Hammers Away at Cost of Section 8 Program." The House manpower and housing subcommittee tortured Assistant Secretary Lawrence B. Simons, the only witness at the hearing. Simons said that the expense is caused by the combination of high housing costs and low tenants' income. He claimed that "In fact, some of the problems eventually encountered in the previous subsidy programs resulted from vastly underestimated costs, from a form of wishful thinking that something could really be gotten for nothing." When members of the committee complained about too many amenities, Simons replied that the amenities were mandated by Congress, and that austere design could lead to poor maintenance, vandalism, vacancies and bad conditions for the residents. "Section 8 projects should be built to last."

The Committee members seemed less concerned about the cost of support for the Existing Housing Section 8 Program, now known as Housing Choice Vouchers. (I use both Section 8 and Vouchers when describing the program, as do most housing professionals and advocates.)

In 1978, President Jimmy Carter said that he believed in the Section 8 Program. Congress grudgingly approved the budget for fiscal 1979 for 400,000 units of Section 8 and public housing. That involved $1.4 billion of contract authority and $31.4 billion in budget authority. (HDR, 1/9/78)

In 1979 the complaints about costs and worries about the economy escalated. Carter's Office of Management and Budget limited funds for HUD. The fiscal 1980 budget request anticipated 300,000 units, with $1.4 billion in contract authority and $29.3 billion in budget authority. Congress estimated that 313,000 units could be developed with reduced funds by shifting more units from new construction to existing housing. The authorization act reflected the estimate of 313,000 units. (HDR, June 11, 1979, page 11). New regulations tightened the rules around costs, limiting amenities and profits while imposing total cost limits. The appropriations committees reduced the estimate to 266,000 units. (HDR, August 6, 1979, page 198).

The trend continued. A Government Accounting Office (GAO) report claimed that Fair Market Rents were too high, a claim that HUD officials disputed. The GAO report claimed that the rents for the new construction program were based on construction and operating costs instead of comparable market rents. To me, it seems odd not to consider actual costs. Again, low balling cost estimates is not the key to success. Fake assumptions about the "market" will not result in feasible development. The GAO report suggested eliminating the new construction program. Instead, public housing and the existing Section 8 program were recommended. Other suggestions included increases in the tenant's contribution to rent. HUD opposed the report and rejected the GAO's recommendations. Congressional hearings again were dominated by questions relating to costs. A good part of the cost increases related to increased interest rates. (HDR March 17, 1980, p. 873-7). The Senate Budget Committee projected 210-236,000 units with the funding level the same as in 1979 (HDR, April 14, 1980, page 948). (HDR June 23, pp. 63-4)

Congress kept giving HUD a very hard time. Housing funds were sent to HUD field offices in the last hours of President Carter's Administration. With a fund reduction, it was estimated that 214, 550 units could be provided. (2/2/81, page 738). All the criticism made the Carter. Administration and Congress reluctant to become ardent defenders of Section 8.

Then came Reagan. Housing groups immediately started to mobilize to fight potential cuts in housing assistance. Cushing Dolbeare, a well-known advocate mentioned in other chapters, was the founder and president of the National Low Income Housing Coalition. When asked about budget cuts, she became even more energetic. "The more the programs are threatened, the larger and more active I would expect our organizations to become." She believed that Congress would keep the programs alive and well, although the electoral defeat of Congressman Thomas (Lud} Ashley was a serious loss.

I knew Cushing as a very effective lobbyist. We differed on one issue. She believed that housing assistance should go only to the very poor, because that was the most serious need. I believed (and still do) that mixed income housing allows everyone in the communities to receive assistance, preventing resentment by tenants who cannot find housing but earn too much to qualify for very low income limits. We both advocated for adequate funds. I admired Cushing's persistence and idealism. She received a McArthur Genius grant and gave all the funds to the Coalition.

Congress kept up the barrage of attacks. Senator William, Armstrong, a Republican from Colorado, wrote a plan calling for a six-month moratorium to study the costs of Section 8. Among the initial recommendations was one to prohibit housing assistance to cities that had rent control. Income limits would be lowered, although that would add to costs. Davis-Bacon would be repealed, allowing lower wages and easier work rules. Sites would be chosen only on the basis of cost. Food stamps and unemployment benefits would be included when calculating tenants' income. Fortunately, housing advocates prevented the implementation of Senator Armstrong's plan. (HDR, April. 27. 1981).

The Reagan Administration took a pretty dim view of subsidized housing. David Stockman, the Director of the Office of Management and Budget (OMB) said that the Section 8 program was a "budget nightmare." (HDR, July 21, 1981, p.130). He strongly advocated cuts to most HUD programs. The HUD Appropriations Committees in Congress had to delay providing funds for HUD in fiscal 1982 until all requested budget cuts were determined. (HDR, September

28, page 26). Another OMB suggestion was to eliminate all FHA insurance programs because private mortgage insurance was available. The GNMA Tandem program was also questioned. Although the public plan was to cut regulations, actual regulatory changes were small, and, even worse, they made financing much more difficult.

People still think that the Section 8 Program for new construction is very expensive. Indeed in 2021, housing development costs in most cities are astronomical. Sticker shock prevails. The lowest construction cost of a two bedroom midrise apartment in New York City in 2021 is about $369,000. (Cumming insights, $461 per square foot, 800 square foot unit). Add at least 25% for fees and other soft costs, and the total cost is $461,000. New York City and San Francisco are especially expensive. On August 27, 2020 New York City Deputy Mayor Vicki Been spoke at a conference of the Citizens' Budget Commission. She said, "We can plan till the cows come home for lower income housing. Until we lower the costs of building, we're not going to get that." That has been a common theme for at least 60 years. Still, costs keep going up. Only Robert Moses was able to lower costs, mostly because of economies of scale. He built thousands of apartments at a time. I was involved in a number of promising plans for lowering costs, but none of them had much of an impact.

IS PRE-FAB THE ANSWER?

I always thought that prefabricated construction might be the answer. Nicholas Lembo, founder and long-term CEO of Manadnock Construction Corp, was the leading prefab builder in New York City. He created prefabricated small homes in a factory located in the Brooklyn Navy Yard. These were nicely designed boxes. They had to be delivered to sites and then hooked up to utilities, saving time, interest and other costs. In 2003 Settlement Housing Fund engaged his company for 37 two family homes in the Ocean Hill-Brownsville area of Brooklyn. The construction cost was about fifty per cent lower than our seven-story building that was planned for Crown Heights, fairly near the prefab development in Brooklyn. This was 2002.

Fast forward to 2021. I called Nick Lembo, whose company had 45 years of experience working in New York City. According to the website, "Affordable housing has always been a cornerstone of our work."

I mentioned Vicki Been's comments and asked him if anything could be done to lower construction costs. He said that something ought to be done, and maybe something could happen in 50 years if the political climate changes. Because of all the requirements that the City Council keeps adding to the Building Code, and because of the cumbersome regulations and procedures of the Building Department, costs keep going in the opposite direction. "New York City is very unfriendly to business."

Nick gave details of excessive code requirements. For example, contractors in New York had always used propane or kerosene heaters at construction sites. Now only electric heaters are permitted, adding unnecessarily to costs. Another example involves tall buildings. Devices must be built so that fire fighters' communications are amplified by a special building system. The cost is $250,000 to $300,000 per installation. A fire captain, visiting one of Monadnock's completed buildings, told Nick that the fire fighters bring their own equipment to reinforce their communications. The fire captain never used the building's system. He didn't even know that such a system existed. He was not speaking for the entire Department.

Workers who live near a new construction site are now required to be hired. The City consequently mandates 30 hours of safety training. Other safety training is also required for various jobs. All this is expensive.

Hiring people from the neighborhoods is not the problem.

"It is the excessive training for a new employee that makes it difficult for people to get work and for us to employ them even for unskilled starting jobs." (Hiring requirements on signs shown below, posted near construction sites throughout New York City)

As of December 1, 2019:

- Workers will not be permitted to work on this site unless they have 30 hours of safety training, demonstrated by an OSHA 30 card, a Limited Site Safety Training Card, or a Site Safety Training Card.

- Workers serving as a Site Safety Manager, Site Safety Coordinator, Concrete Safety Manager, Construction Superintendent or a Competent Person, as required by Section 3301.13.12 of the Building Code, will not be permitted to work on this site unless they have 62 hours of safety training, demonstrated by a Supervisor Site Safety Training Card.

As of September 1, 2020:

- Workers will not be permitted to work on this site unless they have 40 hours of safety training, demonstrated by a Site Safety Training Card.

Visit www.nyc.gov/nycsafety or call 311 for more information.

TO ANONYMOUSLY REPORT UNSAFE CONDITIONS AT THIS WORK SITE, CALL 311.

A partir del 1 de diciembre de 2019:

No se permitirá que los trabajadores trabajen en esta obra a menos que tengan **30 horas de capacitación en seguridad**, demostrada por una tarjeta OSHA 30, una Tarjeta de Capacitación Limitada en Seguridad en la Obra o una Tarjeta de Capacitación en Seguridad en la Obra.

Los trabajadores que se desempeñen como Gerente de Seguridad en la Obra, Coordinador de Seguridad en la Obra, Gerente de Seguridad de Concreto, Superintendente de Construcción o una persona capacitada, según lo requiere la Sección 3301.13.12 del Código de Construcción, no podrán trabajar en esta obra a menos que cuenten con **62 horas de capacitación en seguridad**, demostradas por una Tarjeta de Capacitación en Seguridad en la Obra del Supervisor.

A partir del 1 de septiembre de 2020:

No se permitirá que los trabajadores trabajen en esta obra a menos que tengan **40 horas de capacitación en seguridad**, demostradas por una Tarjeta de Capacitación en Seguridad en la Obra.

Visite www.nyc.gov/nycsafety o llame al 311 para más información.

PARA DENUNCIAR ANÓNIMAMENTE CONDICIONES INSEGURAS EN ESTE SITIO DE TRABAJO, LLAME AL 311.

I mentioned that I never could understand why construction costs were lower in Chicago, where unions were very active. Nick's colleague in Chicago said that developers had a good working relationship with the construction unions, and they were sensitive to keeping costs somewhat lower.

Nick explained how new city requirements have sent the costs spiraling upwards. In 2016 Capsys closed its New York City operations, mainly because the Navy Yard was raising its rent dramatically. Nick was unhappy that "places like the Navy Yard are more interested in movie studios that create jobs for white college-educated young people." Capsys was not valued enough to keep the rents reasonable.

I still think that modular construction could be a significant answer to the high cost problem. Nick and others always told me I was naïve. It was one answer, but not the total answer. He mentioned another modular development that took over two years to build and cost three times as much as it should have. This was Forest City Ratner's B2 building in Brooklyn. "It took about five years to completion. This was after promising 20 to 25 per cent savings in time and cost."

After 45 years as a contractor, Nick admitted to being cynical. He was one of the most honest and effective builders I have ever known.

An article in the December 16, 2020, issue of the New York Times described how modular construction is popular again. It took ten days to build a coronavirus testing center in Bakersfield California for the University of Denver, and one day to set it up. A new 26 story Marriott Hotel in Manhattan is using modular construction and had been expected to open in 2021, prior to the pandemic. It will be the largest modular hotel in the world. Eric Jacobs, chief development officer for Marriot Select Brands in North America is quoted as saying, "we can shave off six months of development." We keep reading in 2021 how it took two weeks to build a hospital in Wuhan to help in China's CoVid medical treatment program. Wow. According to a 2019 report by McKinsey and Company, in America, modular construction can speed up construction by as much as 50 per cent and reduce costs by 20 percent. (NY Times, December 16, 2020, page B7). Still, the process has been around for decades, and costs seem to be going in the opposite direction.

One recent new possibility is the 3D printer. It's hard to imagine, but I read of a 3D printed house with a garage for sale for $299,000 in Riverhead, New York. According to the Builder Pulse Newsletter of January 29, 2021, "Using SQ4D's Autonomous Robotic Construction

System (ARCS), the home was printed on site. The company developed its patent pending ARCS technology to robotically build the footings, foundations, and interior and exterior walls. The proprietary hardware and software enable the construction site to be safer while creating eco-friendly homes at a fraction of the cost.

Built with concrete, the home will deliver strength and durability, but SQ4D also will include a 50-year limited warranty on its 3D-printed structures.

"At $299,999, this home is priced 50% below the cost of comparable newly constructed homes in Riverhead, New York, and represents a major step toward addressing the affordable housing crisis plaguing Long Island," says Stephen King of Realty Connect, the Zillow Premier agent who has the listing."

The house is 1400 square feet and there are two full bathrooms. Could this be one answer?

LOW RISE AND MARK GINSBERG

Over the decades, I struggled to learn about efforts to reduce housing costs. One promising idea was offered by Mark Ginsburg in the eighties. Mark is now a leading affordable housing architect. We thought that a four-story walkup building could work without deep subsidies if a simple amendment to the building code was enacted. A number of us worked together to "reinvent the walkup."

I interviewed Mark recently to discuss that plan. The basic idea was to allow buildings with 2,500 square feet per floor to have only one exit, rather than requiring two. Previously, the requirement for two exits applied to buildings with over 2,000 feet per floor. At the time, we thought that the amendment would make low rise construction much cheaper, adding to housing affordability. After a significant campaign, we were successful in changing the code. Unfortunately, the change did not result in significant cost savings. Furthermore, Mark said that we were at least ten years too late. In the eighties, land was relatively cheap. In the nineties that began to change. Now the price of land has skyrocketed. Today, density is the only answer to feasible development.

Mark recalled the success of the Nehemiah housing initiative in Brooklyn. The sites were very cheap, a prototype housing design was used, and intense supervision resulted in keeping costs down. The local churches provided inexpensive construction loans. This endeavor would be impossible to replicate in New York City today.

Mark echoed Nick Lembo in citing building code changes that add to the cost of housing. He said that it's "always possible to find good reasons to change the code." Who could argue against requiring sprinklers or wheelchair accessibility?"

Mark mentioned the new requirements that are under consideration regarding energy and climate change. These new requirements would add three to five per cent to construction costs. However, at least many of these changes could reduce operating costs.

An op ed article by Justin Gillis in the New York Times on January 25, 2021, lambasted the National Association of Home Builders for "trying to monkey around" with rules that might lower the energy costs of home owners. The article contended that the opposition had to do with the possible reduction in profits. It's more likely that the costs would be passed on to prospective buyers or renters. If energy costs are reduced, so much the better. But, there is a cost involved that has to be considered.

The most recent proposed change in New York City involves prohibiting the use of combustible materials for exterior facades in buildings higher than 75 feet. This was the result of the Grenfield Tower fire in London and other fires outside New York City. Wood super-structures today are no longer possible, although there is renewed interest in laminated wood, also known as mass timber.

Lawsuits by opponents of affordable housing also add to development costs.

"Since 1940, every industry is more productive, except for construction," Mark explained.

He proposed a cost-benefit analysis for changes to the building code. However, he thinks the City Council would be in favor of increases in costs that are supported by the Fire Department or other proponents of safety. "It's hard to argue against the Fire Department."

CORRUPTION AND COST BREAKDOWNS

Luckily, in my fifty years in the housing world, I never encountered corruption personally. One year an intern came back to our office shocked because of what happened at the Building Department. He told us that a building inspector opened his desk drawer, implying that our request for a certificate of occupancy could go very quickly if the right amount of cash were placed in that drawer.

One of my colleagues told me she was depressed because a contractor-developer convinced the subcontractors to inflate their costs, and then shared the inflated amounts fifty-fifty. As I started to write this chapter, I read in the September 30, 2020 edition of Crains New York that it was reported that a former Bloomberg executive pleaded guilty to evading taxes on over $1.4 million in bribes from subcontractors. The bribes were paid in exchange for contracts and subcontracts. Former Turner Construction employees were also allegedly involved. The total in bribes was over $5 million. That disappointed me because of an excellent experience I had with Turner. Turner is a huge corporation with hundreds of employees, and so I hope this was a rare infraction.

Over the decades I would look at construction cost breakdowns that were part of submissions for funding. Contractors had to itemize costs of foundations, superstructures, mechanical costs and dozens of other items. Each contractor seemed to itemize costs in a unique way. It was hard to determine the percentage of total cost that should be attributed to each item, because there was so much variation among contractors. It made me wonder.

MIKE LAPPIN'S SECRETS

There is one person that I admired more than anyone else because of his passion to keep costs as low as possible while still developing or preserving affordable housing. This is Mike Lappin, who was CEO of Community Preservation Corporation, (CPC), for 31 years and is currently active as a developer. Community Preservation Corporation is a major lender to affordable housing owners and has also developed its own portfolio. While Mike was President, the organization completed 95,000 units, mostly renovations with tenants in occupancy. Over my fifty-year involvement in community development, I was never a great fan of acronyms. Still, I had a good one for Mike," ICDIC" which stands for "I can do it cheaper". And indeed he has.

I spoke to him recently, asking how he managed to keep costs so much lower than most other lenders and developers. We spoke of the bank's early achievements in upgrading hundreds of buildings in Washington Heights in Upper Manhattan and in Crown Heights in Brooklyn. Mike was able to save the buildings, insisting that the scope of work consisted of only what was necessary. Still, there was a lot that had to be done, mostly replacing the major mechanical systems of a building. This included plumbing, wiring, heating, elevator, weather tightening the building with new windows, roofs and necessary exterior brick work. Some buildings needed repair of fire escapes, sealing of dumbwaiter shafts and new front doors with intercom systems. A reserve was included in the loans to take care of future needs.

Community Preservation Corporation had control of all operations. Mike would look at a contractor's initial price and then tell the contractor that if the cost could come down, the bank could provide financing fast—really fast. Mike and the staff knew the costs of similar buildings, providing the ability to negotiate effectively. The contractors knew that the bank could act expeditiously. Things could get started within a few months. Getting the funds out quickly was attractive to the contractors. Because there was minimal red tape, prices could be kept lower. And, Mike knew how to play hardball. He could "squeeze the guys."

Most of the buildings were financed through the city's Participation Loan Program. This is a program in which the city provides one per cent loans in combination with private financing. Unlike federal programs, prevailing wages are not mandated. CPC used Section 8 to secure financing only for eight units in each development to avoid the federal prevailing wage requirement.

Mike was able to control planning, design and construction. It seems to me that he lowered costs through sheer will. He never let up.

After the city took direct control of development under the Participation Loan Program, it became more difficult to keep costs down because of increased red tape. New design criteria were not always helpful. In one case, there was a rust around the perimeter of a bathtub. City officials wanted the contractors to remove and replace the tub, instead of just cleaning it up and covering the damaged parts. Pre-construction negotiation caused delay, after delay, and cost went up accordingly. "Process is the hidden factor in costs."

One of Community Preservation Corporation's daunting accomplishments was the renovation of Parkchester, a low-to -moderate income condominium consisting of 271 buildings with 12,271 apartments in the southeast Bronx. Originally built between 1938 and 1941 by Metropolitan Life Insurance Company, by the late nineties the buildings needed major repair, including replacement of plumbing and upgrading electricity for air conditioning. CPC got the job done only with real estate tax exemptions and internal rent subsidies for relatively few residents. Again, the cost was a small fraction of the estimates in 2020 to upgrade public housing.

Mike Lappin remains undaunted. He has a plan for midrise plank construction that can achieve costs that are about two thirds of what large developers are claiming. The plan would use the same design for multiple sites. For some other proposals that Mike has seen, "the prices are disgusting. The system has been hijacked by developers. The true costs have started to decline because of Covid 19, although no one wants to admit it."

VICKI BEEN

In an op ed article in the October 5 edition of Crains, Andrew Rein, the president of the Citizens Budget Commission advocated for revising the zoning and building codes, in order to reduce construction costs. This seemed to be a common theme.

One hopeful trend is the new emphasis on wind, solar and other means of reducing the cost of energy, while reducing the dangers of global warming. This should become the norm in the future without adding much to costs, possibly reducing operating costs dramarically.

As a final exercise, I decided to interview Deputy Mayor Been about costs, recalling her quote at the panel discussion at the Citizens Budget Commission.

I first knew Vicki Been as a promising young lawyer in my late husband's law firm. Then she headed the Furman Center at NYU. Next was a position as Housing Commissioner, and then she became Deputy Mayor to Mayor Bill DeBlasio. I asked her what she would actually do to reduce construction costs. To my surprise, she had some good ideas. Most of our discussion involved cutting red tape.

First and foremost, she stressed the need for political will. She cited an example of a successful response to a crisis. As the Covid 19 pandemic eased in the summer of 2020 in New York City, restaurants were allowed to open with outdoor seating on sidewalks and in parking areas adjacent to the restaurants. The Mayor visited the owner of his favorite restaurant. The owner said that he did not have the time to spend hours at various city offices to get a permit for outdoor seating.

Deputy Mayor Been and her colleagues quickly got to work. They created a one-day permit process, all on line. There were five questions, and a process for self-certification. If there were ambiguities, the restaurant owner could email a photo of the site to make sure that he or she complied with regulations.

People must convey the same kind of urgency to affordable housing, according to Vicki. Why not use video walk throughs for apartment inspections? If luxury tenants find apartments, using videos, why not use these techniques for inspections of affordable housing? This could be followed by in person inspections as needed. Good enforcement and serious penalties for lying would assure compliance without the need to schedule unnecessary on-site inspections.

Deputy Mayor Been has seen examples of ridiculous regulations. For the federal Rental Assistance Demonstration (RAD) program, which allows local housing authorities to provide financing and transfer ownership to private developers, HUD has a regulation that can best be described as crazy. In order to transfer ownership and obtain Section 8 rent subsidies, the owner must restore electrical plates on walls that will be torn down. It would be easy to provide a waiver and prevent expenditures that are totally wasteful. Again, political will is a necessity.

Vicki envisions a concierge desk that could help a builder get a permit immediately if he or she could demonstrate compliance. All this would take leadership and buy-in from everyone who understands the housing crisis and the need for action.

Even though personally I never found answers to the quest to reduce costs, it is a worthwhile pursuit. I do not agree with those who claim that Section 8 is more expensive than other programs. Housing finance today is so complicated that the need for lawyers and accountants has added dramatically to transaction costs. Simplification could lead to overall cost reduction. Having one source of financing could certainly ease the headache factors in development. The best ideas seem to deal with negotiating with contractors and making it easier to obtain permits and approvals. I'm all for that.

CHAPTER 10

Reaganomics and Dwindling HUD Budgets

DRASTIC CUTS, DE-OBLIGATIONS AND recissions were the themes of David Stockman's HUD budget negotiations during the 1980's. In 2021 we have still not recovered.

Forgive me if I whine, but I promise, it's appropriate.

Attacks on Section 8 projects were constant during the Reagan years. Donald Hovde, HUD Undersecretary, added all potential payments for one apartment for 30 years, the length of a Section contract, and screamed about this outrage. He received extensive press coverage. Leon Weiner, a developer and the former Chair of the National Housing Conference said that Hovde's exercise was like adding up all the mortgage payments for a 30-year term and complaining about the over-the-top cost.

There were also a very few scandals about projects that were highlighted in the press. When I asked a favorite reporter to cover a successful development in Harlem, he said that he could envision an article if I could arrange some controversy. I couldn't and wouldn't. The Section 8 housing budget never came near to reaching the levels achieved by Carla Hills during the Ford Administration. Production also never reached her achievements.

However, reductions for the Section 8 program for existing housing, eventually renamed Housing Choice Vouchers, were much less drastic during the Reagan and Bush years

Although I have looked at the reduction of housing funds over the decades, I still find many of the charts at best confusing and at worst misleading. Budget authority often (but not always) includes multiyear calculations. The charts that compare outlays sometimes include expenditures for tenants who have been assisted for years, but do not always examine new levels of assistance. HUD's unit counts for budget, reservations and contract executions did not always match.

Several things are clear. As I write in 2021, three out of every four tenants eligible for Section 8 do not receive Section 8 benefits. Most localities have decades-long waiting lists. The highly touted Low Income Housing Tax Credit Program has produced 90,000 units a year, compared to 200,000 to 400,000 units in the late seventies, days of Section 8 for new construction and substantial rehabilitation, a program eliminated by Reagan.

LEGISLATION AND ADMINISTRATIVE ACTS IN THE EIGHTIES:

In the Budget and Reconciliation Act of 1981, Section 8 was amended to raise the tenants' share of rent to 30 per cent of income. That was a personal defeat for me, because with the help of the late Congressman Ed Koch (before he was Mayor) and the late Senator Jacob Javits, the New York Housing Conference had successfully advocated that tenants pay between 15 and 25 per cent of income for rent, depending on income and family size. This 1981 law seemed to be the beginning of the end. The act also stipulated that 90 per cent of Section 8 assisted apartments be rented to families earning less that 50 per cent of area median income, as opposed to the original 30 per cent requirement, making it difficult for the program to achieve a mix of income groups. The legislation also included a requirement for "modest design." Affordable housing could not include amenities. Heaven forbid.

In February, 1982, Cushing Dolbeare, president of the National Low Income Housing Coalition testified before the House

Banking Committee, stating, that the Reagan Administration's HUD budget cut was "by far the largest proposed for any activity of the federal government." However, because of the negative press, many witnesses at the hearing acquiesced to the Administration's proposal to eliminate all funding for Section 8 new construction or substantial rehabilitation, except for Section 202 housing for the elderly. (HDR, March 29, 1982, page 859). In a May 13 memorandum, the main HUD office in Washington directed the field offices to cancel projects that were "low priority." The 1982 Supplemental Appropriations bill effectively cut off new allocations of Section 8 funding for 1982. (HDR, June 21, 1982, page 45.)

Yes, that was terrible. But I was also annoyed that HUD eliminated the availability of higher Fair Market Rents for recently completed buildings, a regulation that my colleague, John Maguire, and I has invented to rescue Manhattan Plaza, described in chapter 8.

Very serious damage had been done in the Budget and Reconciliation Act of 1981. More drastic budget reductions would soon follow.

For some reason I kept the Congressional Record that contained the House Budget Reconciliation Act passed on November 18, 1983. Title II, Section 209 marks the formal death toll of the Section 8 program for new construction and substantial rehabilitation. New projects would not be permitted after January 1, 1984. There would be a new program for moderate rehabilitation, one that would become haunted by scandals while Samuel Pierce was Secretary.

However, at least the Section 8 Program for existing housing remained intact. However, Reagan's first proposed budget for fiscal 1984 included only $515 million for housing, a huge cut from the $8.4 billion that Congress had passed for 1983. There were counter proposals, including the use of funds left from prior years and using shorter contract terms to estimate costs. HUD also proposed changing the calculation of Fair Market rents, using the 40th percentile of private rents. Congressmen from New York objected, fearing that the rents would be too low, leading to abandonment. (P.1025,HDR, 4/25/83.) Eventually, HUD compromised, using the 45th percentile of recent movers. The Section 8 Existing Housing Program was renamed as the Housing Choice Voucher Program. The final Act included $9.93 billion in budget authority. However, the target of 61,220 units was not reached. Only 36,147 units were reserved, mostly because of funding delays.

The next year HUD's target was increased to 87,500 units, using recaptured funds. The Appropriations bill provided for only 25,000 additional Vouchers.

Rules became more stringent. All families with vouchers could earn no more than 50 per cent of area median income. Several deductions were eliminated. The spirit of generosity was certainly missing in action. Congress kept arguing and asking questions about the Voucher program. Would landlords be receptive? Would some of the new rules force tenants to pay more than 30 per cent of income for rent? (HRD, April 9, 1984, p.956)

The final Appropriations Act for 1985 provided 38,500 incremental vouchers. (HDR, July1, 1984, p.96). The OMB budget requested increasing the number of incremental vouchers to 150,000 for 1986. The enlarged program was the "keystone" HUD program. (HDR, September 24, 1984, p. 331). However, the final 1986 HUD appropriations bill resulted in only 36,000 incremental vouchers. (HDR, November 18, 1985, p. 495). If the process seems crazy and confusing, that's because it is.

Just to make things worse, The Gramm-Rudman Act, officially the Balanced Budget and Emergency Deficit Control Act of 1985, provided for automatic funding cuts if the president and Congress could not agree to reach targets. This was very worrisome. State and local officials tried to find resources to make up for the loss.

HOMELESSNESS AND CRISES:

The serious budget cuts occurred in the 1980's just when homelessness started to become a major problem in urban areas. I will not claim that the decline of federal funds for housing caused homelessness. There were other forces at work in many areas of the country. In New York some of the other factors included the emptying of facilities for the mentally ill, public assistance rents that were totally inadequate, conversion of single room occupancy buildings to luxury use, individuals still returning from Vietnam military service, individuals released from prisons and rising rents.

However, lack of federal assistance for housing certainly added dramatically to homelessness, which had not been prevalent in the seventies. There were other serious problems, including overcrowding, dilapidated housing, and so-called flophouses. In New York City, entire families were crowded into one hotel room if the family was receiving public assistance. But no one was living on the streets until the eighties. No matter what, the lack of significant federal assistance for housing certainly did not help.

On October 22, 1986, President Reagan signed the Tax Reform Act of 1986, which included the Low Income Housing Tax Credit Program. This program became the major vehicle for affordable housing development, with section 8 used only for the lowest income brackets. Still, Section 8 Vouchers remained important for privately owned buildings and to make the Tax Credit program feasible. Financing affordable housing became increasingly complex. It still is.

MORE LEGISLATION:

In 1987, the first budget proposal called for 50,000 vouchers. The Appropriations bills had the same estimate, although recaptured funds were part of the equation.

The Voucher budget kept trickling up-with 79,000 proposed for fiscal 1988. Funds to address homelessness were included. The Iran-contra dispute left little time for consideration of housing issues. (HDR, June 13, 1987, page 133).

On March 28, 1988, a federal task force released a report entitled," A Decent Place to Live." The Task Force was headed by Senator Alphonse D'Amato, the conservative Republican from New York and Senator Alan Cranston, the Democrat from California who headed the Housing Subcommittee for many years. "Of the 129 million low-income renter households in 1983, only 28 per cent benefited from federal housing programs." The task force set forth a 10-point plan with the goal of livable affordable housing by the year 2,000. The plan combined production, tax incentives and rental subsidies.

A second panel, sponsored by the Advisory Commission on Intergovernmental Relations, claimed that the lack of affordable housing was the "root cause of homelessness." Deep cuts in the HUD budgets was a major problem.

The campaign platform for the Democratic Party in the 1988 elections affirmed support for decent housing for all Americans and called for an end to homelessness. "There is no good reason why the nation we love, the greatest and richest nation on earth, should rank first...in the percentage of total expenditures devoted to defense but nearly last in the percentage devoted to education and housing." (HDR, June 25, 1988, p. 196) The candidates, Michael Dukakis and Lloyd Bentsen, alas, were not elected.

CONFUSING CHARTS:

The only good news is that HUD continued to extend Section 8 funding to cover existing commitments. Budget authority declined dramatically over the years mainly because the program that provided 20 to 30-year commitments for new construction ended. Many charts that show year-to-year commitments are confusing. The National Low Income Housing Coalition's Table 8 in "Changing Priorities, 1976-2007," showed a decline of housing assistance compared to the total budget between 1976 and 2002. Table 9 shows that housing subsidies declined 59 per cent during the same period.

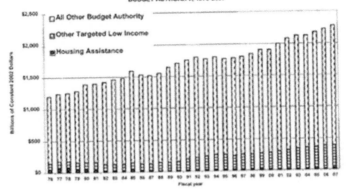

GRAPH 8. LOW INCOME HOUSING, OTHER TARGETED LOW INCOME, AND TOTAL BUDGET AUTHORITY, 1976-2007

Graph 8 indicates that the housing assistance budget authority trend is in the opposite direction as previously indicated, while budget authority for other low income assistance and for the total federal budget increased (see Appendix B, Table 4).

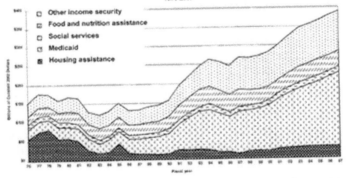

GRAPH 9. BUDGET AUTHORITY FOR TARGETED LOW INCOME PROGRAMS 1976-2007

Graph 9 shows that budget authority for low income housing was the largest low income assistance program until 1981, which is when the most severe cuts to housing assistance occurred. Between 1976 and 2002:

- Housing assistance budget authority fell by 59%.
- Medicaid budget authority increased by 493%.
- Other income security budget authority increased by 179%.
- Food and nutrition assistance budget authority increased by 76%.
- Social services budget authority increased by 3%.

Changing Priorities . 2002 . 7

When I asked if there were updated charts, Ed Gramlich from the Coalition staff referred me to Douglas Rice, a Senior Fellow at the center on Budget and Policy Priorities. He was "not a fan" of the Coalition's chart. He wrote to me that that "the period from the mid-1970's to the mid-1990's is actually 'a golden era' of federal housing aid," He added that "the real decline/ stagnation in federal housing policy began in the mid-1990's and has continued to this day. He sent me a link to a chartbook with 13 charts and 7 tables. I read his November,2020 article that described the shortfall of Section 8 Vouchers during the crisis period of the pandemic "when millions are struggling to pay rent."

Again, there always had seemed to be no danger that existing tenants would be cut off from assistance. And then came the Budget Control Act of 2011, which required automatic budget cuts, beginning in 2013. The cuts were known as "sequestration." Douglas Rice wrote on November 6, 2013 that "Sequestration could cut Housing Vouchers for as many as 185,000 families by the end of 2014." Families could lose their assistance for the first time since the beginning of the Section 8 program.

When the New York Housing Conference circulated a letter to Congress protesting sequestration, representatives of 90 organizations signed on. Included were nonprofit organizations, banks, developers, managers and more. New York City started to establish procedures that would allow lower rents for Section 8 assisted apartments, but the protests were intense.

The Budget Act of 2014 added some support back. However, an editorial in the March 22, 2014 New York Times claimed that less than half the Vouchers lost in 2013 were being replaced. Although sequestration has not been repealed, there have been exceptions every year. No one who had Section 8 has been forced on to the streets.

Just to add to the confusion actual outlays and households assisted keeps increasing. An article in ANNALS of the American Academy of Political and Social Science, 686, by Robert Collinson, Ingrid Gould Ellen and Jens Ludwig includes a chart that shows the increases. Over $150 billion was spent in 2010, which sounds like a lot.

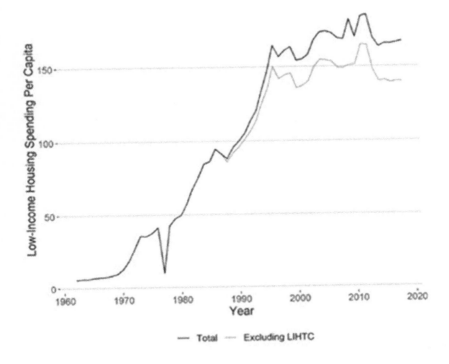

— Total — Excluding LIHTC

Still, today only one out of every four eligible households receives housing assistance. President Joseph Biden's campaign in 2020 included $640 billion over ten years for housing. To my delight, he would require the Voucher program to become an entitlement. I am not sure that the budget authority is adequate, but it is unlikely that every eligible tenant will use the program. The Biden plan, if enacted, would certainly be an amazingly great start. Plus, there would be a renters' tax deduction for middle income households. If the skeptics are wrong and Congress actually cooperates, we could see an end to the housing crisis that has existed in America for as long as I can remember.

CHAPTER 11

What do Tenants Say?

As an advocate and as former head of a nonprofit housing owner, I was well aware that the Section 8 Program, as important as it is, needed some tweaks at the very least. Thirty per cent of income is a lot for low-income tenants to pay for housing, especially for families with children. As a nonprofit owner, it was aggravating when city agencies took months to approve vacant apartments for eligible tenants. Even when we lost money, however, I always said that I wish we had more Section 8 Vouchers to complain about.

As I was nearing the end of this book, I realized that the most important opinion was that of the tenants who are assisted by Section 8. They are the reason for doing anything at all when it comes to housing. I decided to interview a few tenants. Two would reside in Settlement Housing Fund's largest development in the Bronx. I decided to reach out to colleagues and to the staff of the Low Income Housing Coalition to find tenants in other areas of the country. The Coalition provided three names, two of whom lived in project-based Section 8 buildings and one who had a Housing Choice Voucher. One lived in New Jersey and one in Florida. Also recommended by the Coalition was one New York resident, but she refused to talk with me because I had good things to say about several CEOs of the New York City Housing Authority. However, another tenant from Florida gave me the name of her colleague, a resident of a development for senior citizens in New York. Ironically, this was a building that I had worked hard to develop in the eighties. I also reached out to Steve Norman, who heads the Kings County Housing Authority in Seattle. His staff introduced me to two tenants who are included. The following seven short interviews follow the order of the day or the interview.

The results of the interviews were surprising. The tenants all had strong opinions and had lived through some negative experiences. One tenant complained about extremely poor maintenance in project-based Section 8 buildings, but she did not want to be quoted about the specific developments. Overall, the outcomes were positive.

INTERVIEW WITH MS. SHALONDA RIVERS

Ms. Shalonda Rivers is the President of the 22 Avenue Apartments Cordoba Tenants Association in Opa Locka of Miami, Dade County, Florida. She has been in the Section 8 program since she moved to the building with her four children in 2001. This is a multifamily building that benefits from Tax Credits and project-based Section 8. The neighborhood is predominantly low-income. Ms. Rivers is a proud advocate for tenants and is on the boards of the National Low Income Housing Coalition and the National Alliance of HUD tenants.

She was not on a long waiting list for Section 8. It took only two months for her to be approved and to move to her apartment.

The neighborhood is problematic. Ms. Rivers sent her children to schools in a different neighborhood. One of her sons went to a school to a predominantly Spanish school with Spanish speaking students. Her son actually benefitted. He had his classes in Spanish and is bilingual.

The best thing about Housing Choice Vouchers is that there is a choice. People can take their Vouchers and move to another building or another neighborhood.

Ms. Rivers has a lot of suggestions for changes. She believes that residents should learn about "home buying programs." She thinks that HUD should be required to provide opportunities for tenants to get out of poverty. "A direct in-house home buyer incentive should be attached to the tenant lease or agreement."

Furthermore, development agreements should be monitored and enforced. The Tax Credit agreement for her building included provisions for computer labs, nutrition classes, job training and more. A nutritionist came to the property for about two weeks and never returned.

Management is also a concern. Managers do not comply with tenant selection regulations. For example, the managers approved several people with records of felonies, counter to HUD regulations. There are many other problems in her building. The laundry facility is very bad, and there are structural issues.

Ms. Rivers believes that the Section 8 Program should set priorities for tenant selection according to need. She recently noticed a father with children who were living in a van. That should not happen. Families with serious needs should come first when allocating subsidies.

Ms. Rivers was most gracious. I heard her speaking to someone on the building staff about a repair, and she was polite and respectful. She is passionate about the importance of "decent, safe and sanitary" housing.

INTERVIEW WITH MS. YANIRA CORTES

Ms. Yanira Cortes has been receiving Section 8 Voucher Choice assistance since September, 2018. She lives with her four children in a beautiful 3-bedroom home in Ocean County, New Jersey. She works for the Home Energy Assistance program in Ocean County. She is also finishing her college degree, taking classes at night.

She was not always so fortunate.

From 2011 until 2018 Ms. Cortes lived in a rat-infested, substandard apartment in the Newark area. The unit had mold and needed a gut rehabilitation, even though the owner benefited from project-based Section 8. The building received a "zero" rating from HUD's REAC inspections. Still, HUD did nothing to alleviate the situation. Ms. Cortes organized the residents and went to meet with all the elected and appointed government officials. She also met with local HUD officials. She worked nonstop. She received help from former State Senator Jennifer Beck, and from the NAACP. She obtained a pro bono attorney who helped her start a class action lawsuit. With the help of many, she obtained her Section 8 Voucher. At first she could not find adequate housing for her family, and she turned down buildings in poor condition or in dangerous neighborhoods.

Finally, she found the home where she lives now. The home has front and back yard spaces where her children (ages 6,8,9 and 12) can play safely. They attend a very good school nearby, (a public school). When Ms. Cortes speaks about her house, one can hear how happy she is. It's like listening to music.

She calls her Voucher "Temporary Section 8," because she knows that renewal after two years depends on federal appropriations. She worries about what could happen if the funds are not provided by Congress. Even though her attorney tells her not to worry, the fact that the Voucher could possibly expire is cause for concern.

Ms. Cortes has helped to organize residents in other buildings that are substandard. She is concerned about the building where her mother lives, mainly because of mold. She hopes that with enough organizing, her mother can find a better home. She has to fight very hard to make anything good happen. She stressed the importance of never giving up.

Ms. Cortes thinks that the best thing about Section 8 is that tenants have the opportunity to move to a better place. She was happy to leave Essex County and move to Ocean County.

The worst thing about the program is that some areas have very bad administration. Some administrators do not even try to monitor the conditions of assisted buildings. The case worker in the county where her mother lives pays no attention to problems. It was very hard for her mother to report a decline in income recently. In Ms. Cortes' county, the case worker was very cooperative when Ms. Cortes had to stop working because of Covid 19. The case worker changed the Section 8 agreement almost immediately. Ms. Cortes got to know a few HUD officials when she was reporting substandard conditions in her previous building. Ms. Cortes had good things to say about Lynne Patton, the former Regional Administrator in the New York/New Jersey Region, which also includes Puerto Rico and the U.S. Virgin Islands.

Ms. Cortes spoke about other problems. She mentioned that some landlords do not accept Section 8 tenants. Others brand Section 8 recipients unfairly. Ms. Cotes is very grateful, because without Section 8, she could have ended up homeless.

Ms. Cortes thinks that the Voucher program should provide permanent assistance as long as it is needed by the tenants. She thinks that Section 8 should be available for everyone who cannot afford decent housing without assistance.

After Ms. Cortes finishes college, she would like to be a code inspector. "I like to help people," she told me.

INTERVIEW WITH GERALDINE COLLINS

Geraldine Collins is from South Carolina but has lived in New York City for 45 years. She was married to a real estate broker/developer. They owned a brownstone on the Upper West Side of Manhattan. After her husband was diagnosed with three different cancers and had several operations, their savings were depleted. They lost their brownstone, and they had to move.

In 2004, they moved into Phelps House a federally subsidized Section 202 building for senior citizens, handicapped and mobility impaired individuals located on Columbus Avenue and West 89 Street. This building is owned by New Goddard Riverside, a subsidiary of Goddard Riverside Neighborhood Center. Settlement Housing Fund was the consultant in the early eighties, fighting many battles to obtain a federal Section 202 loan with project-based Section 8. I worked hard and long to get the building financed and completed. HUD did not usually include a community center in a 202 building, and it took a lot of work to get the idea accepted.

I was very sad to learn that Mr. and Mrs. Collins experienced difficulties because of poor management. When they first moved in, there were leaks under the kitchen sink, and the cabinet under the sink had actually rotted.

Mr. and Mrs. Collins had never been smokers. When they complained about the unpleasant smoke odor throughout the apartment, they asked if any other apartment was available. Management said "no." Mrs. Collins suffers from respiratory issues, and Mr. Collins was in stage four cancer. He later died—within five months of moving into Phelps House.

Luckily, Goddard changed management twice since 2004. The present management company, Grenadier Realty, is doing a great job.

Mrs. Collins suffered through many difficulties. Her husband passed away in 2004, and then her mom 2005. She had to move her dad to live with her after her mom died. Her father lived with her in a one-bedroom apartment until his death in October 2010.

Amazingly, in spite of Mrs. Collins' disabilities, she became a housing advocate and tenant leader. She formed a tenant association and is now President of the Phelps House Tenants Association. Through her years of organizing, she is now President of The National Alliance of HUD Tenants that advocates on behalf of 1.7 million HUD tenants throughout the country. She goes to Washington DC, 3 to 4 times a year and meets with HUD officials and members of Congress to help to enforce better policies within HUD. Shalonda Rivers is one of Mrs. Collins board members.

Mrs. Collins believes that everyone who needs section 8 should receive assistance. She thinks that if operated properly by management, any section 8 housing property can be a decent and safe place to live. HUD should be more rigorous in its inspection process. There are tenants living in mold, mildew, and rodent-infested buildings. Under these circumstances, the landlord should be held accountable for not keeping the property habitable for low-income tenants. She thinks that 30% of gross income is not too much for rent, if based on a person receiving Social Security and pension. However, she believes that It is ridiculous that HUD includes a person's life insurance policy as an asset when calculating one's rent.

Geraldine Collins has committed herself in the fight to end homelessness, "one family at a time". Her goal is to help end homelessness in the United States.

INTERVIEW WITH RAMON CEPADA AND DENISSE CEPADA

A few years ago, I interviewed Ramon Cepada, who lives in New Settlement Apartments, a complex of 20 buildings that was a subject of my other book, Neighborhood Success Stories. His apartment was immaculate and tastefully furnished. He was very proud of his two children, both of whom had achieved outstanding academic success. I decided to interview him for this book, because I knew he had experience with Section 8. Because of the pandemic, this interview, like all the others, was by phone. Anticipating complicated questions, Mr. Cepada wanted his daughter, Denisse, to be present. She was a great translator and very helpful.

Mr. Cepada lived at New Settlement from 1992 until 1998 and then again from 2002 until the present.

Mr. Cepada believes that Section 8 is important because it provides security, helping tenants to be able to pay the rent. Because of good timing, he was not on a long waiting list.

When I asked about the worst part of the program, he spoke about problems with the new management, and a neighboring tenant who threw garbage carelessly. He thought that tenant selection was not is rigorous as it should be. He did not say anything negative about his experience with his Voucher.

Because of problems with management, sometimes he thinks he would like to move. However, he had no issues with the neighborhood in the Bronx.

Mr. Cepada believes that Section 8 should be available for everyone who cannot afford market rate rents. He thinks middle income people should be included, and that income limits should be increased. He had been worried that if his daughter had wanted to share his apartment, their combined income would be too high. However, Denisse Cepada decided to live in her own apartment.

Mr. Cepada did not want to talk about himself. Denisse, however, said that he was a very attentive and caring father. He remains very protective of his family. Her enthusiasm was genuine and palpable.

INTERVIEW WITH MARIA VENTURA

Maria Ventura lives in Kings County, the area surrounding Seattle, Washington. After several jobs, she was working as a waitress. She had a severe work accident, that left her with spine and hands problems, as well as the need for a walker. She did not get any treatment or compensation. In fact, she became homeless. Her sister, Mirna Leon, referred her to the Sophia Way, an organization that runs a shelter and advocates for homeless women. Sophia Way referred her to the Kings County Housing Authority. A few weeks later, she was offered an apartment at the Discovery Heights in IIssaquah, Washington. This is a project-based Section 8 development.

It was amazing to talk to Maria. She is one of the most positive, upbeat people I have ever encountered. She thinks that Section 8 is a great program, providing good housing for people "without much income." She has lived in her current apartment since May,2018. She did not have to be on a long waiting list, although she hears from others who did have a difficult time finding an affordable place to live. Maria kept talking about how lucky she is. Her apartment is beautiful, in a "wealthy neighborhood," where apartments like hers might cost $1,800 a month. She has a beautiful view and enjoys looking at the trees. When I asked whether she would prefer another apartment or neighborhood, her answer was "no way."

I asked her to tell me what was the worst thing about Section 8. She hesitated and then said that everyone was not as lucky as she was. Some people were on a waiting list for three years or more. She also said that she heard people discriminate against those who receive Section 8, looking down on them. She told me about the negative comments of people in the waiting room at her doctor's office.

Personally, she had no problems with negative reactions. All she had to do was to describe the classes she was taking at Bellevue College. Then people "treat her better".

Maria is ecstatic about Bellevue College. In fact, she is number one in her class. She is taking classes to learn computer skills and to study art. However, after she gets her B.A., she wants to go on to law school and become a lawyer.

She speaks highly of the staff at the building. However, there is one person she avoids. This staff member tried to tell her that she would have to leave because she was a full-time student and not eligible for Section 8. That rule only applies to students under 24, whose parents earn too much to qualify for the program. Maria was able to get a letter from the college that she was a part time student. Furthermore, when Maria said she was studying to become a lawyer and that she had access to legal help, the staff member backed away and never said another word about Maria's status.

Maria believes that Section 8 should be available to everyone who needs housing assistance.

Her enthusiasm about her apartment and the college courses was inspiring. Maria is writing a book in English and Spanish, illustrated with her artwork.

INTERVIEW WITH JOENAY PALMER

Joenay Palmer lives with her daughter in Federal Way, South Kings County, Washington.

She started living by herself when she was 18, and "never had a stable place to stay." She became homeless and went to a very uncomfortable shelter, with rats and miserable conditions. Because she has a disability, the Department of Rehabilitation referred her to Federal Way.

Joenay is very grateful for Section 8. She wants the best of everything for her daughter. She loves her home, and the neighborhood. Her daughter goes to an excellent school. She said that her neighbors are nice and very friendly. "God has blessed me," she told me, several times.

Because of her disability, she did not need to be on a long waiting list.

Joenay is hoping to save enough money to buy a home. Because of the stability from Section 8 and job training and coaching from another program, she managed to open her own business—a day care facility that she operates in a nearby home that she rents.

In her thoughts, Section 8 is a "stepping stone" that will enable her to buy a home. She is working hard to make a profit after paying all the expense at the day care center. At the same time, she worries about making too much money that will make her ineligible for Section 8.

She has a very positive attitude and cares passionately about assuring that her daughter has opportunities and "the best life possible."

Joenay believes that Section 8 should be available for everyone who cannot afford private housing. The one change she would like to see would be an incentive for home ownership. "The goal should be to upgrade," not to be always dependent on government assistance. In the meantime, she kept describing how lucky she is that for nine years, she and her daughter have a stable home because of Section 8.

INTERVIEW WITH JANE TERRY

Jane Terry had to move to a homeless shelter because of her troubled marriage. She adhered to all the rules at the shelter and received priority for permanent housing. She first moved to New Settlement Apartments in 1990 and received Section 8 to supplement her public assistance payments so that she could afford the rent. New Settlement is Settlement Housing Fund's large scale restoration of what had been an abandoned neighborhood in the Bronx. The staff at New Settlement advised Jane about literacy programs. Jane went to the public library, obtained her Graduate Equivalency Degree and studied to become a registered nurse. As her income went up, she no longer qualified for Section 8. That was the good news. However, after retiring, her income from Social Security was insufficient, and her Section 8 payments were restored. That was also the good news.

Jane Terry describes Section 8 as "a bridge that helps those who are struggling, enabling them to avoid becoming homeless." Often working people cannot attend to the needs of their children if they have to pay too much of their earnings for rent. Section 8 is a very "helpful bridge."

When I asked if she liked her home, she said "I love it." She lives on the third floor of a walk-up, and wishes she had the use of an elevator. She said the neighborhood is "just fine."

I asked her what was the worst thing about the Section 8 program. She said that has heard of other buildings that do not provide adequate services and suffer from inadequate supervision of landlords.

She would change the program to incorporate access to social workers. Some would help families deal with the educational needs of their children. She said it would be especially helpful if senior citizens had the assistance of social workers so they could deal with doctors' appointments and other issues that affect people as they grow older.

Jane Terry believes that Section 8 should be available for all who need help—that special bridge—so they can afford to rent a decent place to live. She likes the idea of assisting middle income families who cannot afford market rate rentals.

I learned a lot from these interviews. It would be a good idea for government officials to describe opportunities (if any) for affordable home ownership. I was surprised to hear about poor maintenance in Section 8 developments, because the ones I had visited were in excellent repair. Everyone agreed that Section 8 should be vastly expanded.

CHAPTER 12

My Somewhat Humble Recommendations for the Future

CLARA FOX, WHO WAS my boss for 14 years and originally a Section 8 skeptic, said that "Section 8 should be an entitlement. It should be like Medicare or Social Security—a program available for everyone who qualifies, and something that the federal government cannot take away." I agreed immediately and still do 45 years later. When I suggested that kind of expansion to housing advocates, beginning in the late 1970's and lasting until the last few months, the "realists" would scold me. Amazingly, members of Congress are now seriously considering a plan that would make Section 8 available for all eligible tenants. President Joseph Biden included this four-fold expansion as part of his campaign. The phrase "universal Section 8" has become popular among advocates. It would be great if every eligible tenant could benefit from Section 8. New appropriations and regulations could even come close to realizing the goal of the Housing Act of 1949: "A decent home and a suitable living environment for every American family." I have thoughts about eventually expanding eligibility for the program. But for now, in 2021, it would be miraculous if universal Section 8 is included in President Biden's planned Infrastructure Act. Even better, it would be fantastic if the proposed act is passed by Congress.

In the spirit of "nothing is perfect," I do have suggestions for tweaking and expanding the program, allowing Section 8 to become even more helpful to tenants, property owners and communities. In the meantime, it will be important to read the new Biden statute, word for word, and the regulations to assure that the program is workable. Details matter. Furthermore, local agencies need to start planning as soon as possible so that administration can be relatively seamless.

Thinking ahead, my ideal program would include the revisions that follow.

INCLUDE MODERATE-AND MIDDLE-INCOME TENANTS

First, I would change the eligibility for Section 8 to include moderate and middle-income tenants who cannot afford market rate housing. If tenants cannot afford HUD's Fair Market Rent with 25 per cent of income, they would become eligible. In New York City, San Francisco and many other areas, rents have "gone through the roof" according to a recent NYU study. The share of renters who pay over 30 per cent of their income for rent was 25 per cent in 1960 and close to 50 per cent in 2016. (Through the Roof, Furman Center, page 3). Middle-income families could become resentful if all low income families lived in decent housing, while higher income families were forced to pay extremely high rents or reside in poor, overcrowded homes. Middle-income people (like low-income people) work hard, have children to feed, bills to pay and often pay more than 30 per cent of their income for housing. If middle-income families received Section 8 benefits, there would be a significant constituency for the program. It might actually become an entitlement. I could envision a process that allowed Section 8 to become part of the nondiscretionary budget classification, assuring adequate funding every year.

GOODBYE STIGMAS

In other countries, middle income tenants are eligible for government support.

At a recent seminar sponsored by New York's Citizens Housing and Planning Council, the topic was public housing in Vienna.

Viennese housing officials (on Zoom) explained that 80 per cent of the residents of Vienna are eligible for subsidized housing. They emphasized that there is no stigmatization of those who are subsidized. In Singapore, 82 per cent of the population live in ethnically and economically diverse public housing. I visited the projects, and they are beautiful. In most of the developments owned by Settlement Housing Fund in New York, the tenant population has a mix of incomes ranging from formerly homeless levels to middle-income. We were able to use New York City capital grants to make rents affordable for middle and moderate-income families, while using Vouchers for formerly homeless families. The housing developments are still thriving thirty to forty years after initial occupancy. The waiting lists include middle income households.

Eva Rosen, Assistant Professor at Georgetown University, wrote a book entitled, The Voucher Promise. She lived for a year in the Park Heights neighborhood in Baltimore, where many Voucher holders are able to find housing. She interviewed home owners, landlords, and tenants. Residents with Vouchers had to endure serious stigmatization. The home owners were sure that the value of their properties had skydived because of the Section 8 renters who live in the neighborhood. Some of the neighborhood residents and property owners interviewed by Professor Rosen looked down on Section 8 renters. But on the whole, in spite of these issues, Professor Rosen concluded that Voucher holders did much better than low-income families who did not have rent subsidies. Their housing was decent, and they were more secure.

Several of the tenants whom I interviewed in the previous chapter spoke either about feeling stigmatized or knowing others who were stigmatized.

Would the expansion of the program to cover middle-income tenants help? I believe that it would not only end the stigma but would also provide an important benefit for middle income tenants who want to live in cities.

I inadvertently embarrassed my colleagues in March, 2021 at a New York Housing Conference Zoom meeting with Congressman Richie Torres. He made an excellent presentation about the expansion of temporary housing benefits in the American Rescue

Act of 2021, and said he was planning to support a bill to make Section 8 available for all eligible tenants. I asked whether he would ever consider expanding the program to cover moderate and middle-income families. He answered politely, but such an expansion did not seem to be high on his priority list. The question surprised some of the members of the Conference leadership. Why in the world did I bring up such an idea? At least my critics laughed after the meeting. However, that does not mean that I was wrong. Section 8 assistance should be available to everyone who needs assistance. Since about 66 per cent of Americans own their homes according to the Census, participation in Section 8 by middle income tenants would not necessarily add dramatically to costs. In fact, because they would need less subsidy than low-income tenants, the per person cost would go down.

LOWER THE RENTS THAT TENANTS PAY

Even more radical, I would decrease the tenants' contribution to rent from 30 per cent of income to a range from 15 to 25 per cent of income, depending on family size. Until the Reagan Administration, the standard for rent in affordable housing or in calculating home ownership expenses was 25 per cent of income and less for large families. One week's salary each month was the guideline for mortgage lending. Still, even 25 per cent was often a difficult burden for families. The "George Healy Act", passed by Congress in 1936, stipulated that the income of a family could not exceed five times the rent, or six times for large families. (Elizabeth Wood, Fifty years of Public Housing in America). Six times was also the ratio for the Mitchell Lama program in New York City and New York State. Today, it can be very hard for a family with children to make ends meet while paying 30 per cent of income for rent. As I described in chapter 4, the New York Housing Conference, working with Congressman Edward Koch, successfully added an amendment to the legislation that established Section 8 in 1974, reducing the tenants' share of rent to 15 per cent for large families. From 1974 until 1983, the tenant contribution to rent for Section

8 ranged from 15 to 25 per cent of adjusted income. The Reagan Administration raised the contribution for all tenants to 30 per cent of income in a budget reconciliation act. I am always surprised that today very few housing professionals know that 30 per cent of income for rent is a fairly new standard.

Often when I criticize the 30 per cent requirement, policy leaders will tell me that most people pay at least that much, and low-income families and individuals pay a whole lot more. Rents in many cities have increased dramatically in recent years, while the incomes of all but the very wealthy have stagnated.

The authors of Through the Roof (p.9), an NYU Furman Center publication, claimed that many people believe it is easier for middle-income families to pay over 30 per cent of income for rent than it is for very low-income tenants. The theory is that that middle income families still have enough money left over to cover other expenses after devoting over 30 per cent of income for rent. However, middle income renters pay higher taxes and do not qualify for some benefits available to lower income families. A range of 15 to 25 per cent of income would be best for all.

WE NEED TO BUILD MORE AFFORDABLE HOUSING

At last, I think I have one recommendation that most housing advocates will support. Section 8 expansion will be successful only if there is an adequate housing supply.

One very helpful legislative change would be to re-invent the Section 8 new construction and substantial rehabilitation program. The program would resemble the one that was originally enacted in 1974. Fair Market Rents would be established using cost indices to establish rents needed to cover debt service, reserves, and operating costs. There would be separate Fair Market Rents for high-rise buildings, low-rise buildings and substantial rehabilitation of existing structures. Section 8 contracts could be pledged to obtain financing. However, the Section 8 contracts would be automatically renewable. The contract term should be the same as the term of the permanent mortgage used for financing.

In 1975, I mentioned to a few housing professionals that I was worried about forty-year FHA-insured mortgages combined with twenty-year Section 8 contracts. What would happen after 20 years? Everyone laughed at me. One lawyer told me not to worry because "they will only evict the elderly and the handicapped." It seemed unthinkable to everyone except me that the contracts would not be automatically extended, probably with rent increases that would reflect costs. But, in the nineties, when many contracts did expire, there were problems galore. Elaborate new programs were invented to create new contracts that were "marked up or marked down to market." The result was a program with very high rents (supported by "Enhanced" Vouchers) in neighborhoods that had improved dramatically, and rents that were too low in poor neighborhoods. It would have been better to extend the Section 8 contracts with rents that reflected increased operating costs and, in some cases, new mortgages. State or locally financed Section 8 buildings had 40 year contracts, and special "deals" were made when contracts expired.

Luckily, many Section 8 projects remained in the program. In New York, the City often provided incentives to developers so they would remain in the program at the end of the Section 8 contracts. In my newly imagined project-based section 8 program, owners would have an incentive to stay in the program, because rents would be adjusted annually to reflect operating costs. It might also be advisable to require owners to pay a stiff penalty if they refused to renew a Section 8 contract.

HOUSING NOSTALGIA

I have great memories of working on early project-based Section 8 developments. The one-stop shopping experience was a good one. The New York Area Office would review the FHA insured financing and the Section 8 contract simultaneously. The process would take months instead of years. We did not have to piece together multiple sources of financing that had regulations that conflicted with one another. We really do need to revive the original Section 8 program for new construction and substantial rehabilitation.

In the meantime, we should use the Housing Trust Fund, Low Income Tax Credits, state and local subsidies, the programs of the Federal Home Loan Bank, and philanthropic grants to produce as much affordable housing as possible as soon as possible. We must also build more housing for seniors, the fastest growing part of the population. The New York Times on April 4, 2021 quoted a Harvard study stating that nearly ten million retirement-age households spent over 30 per cent of income on housing. New housing for seniors is urgent. If new public housing could happen, that would be great too. It should be possible to combine these programs with the revived Section 8 Voucher Program.

The need is urgent. Another Harvard study described the loss of low rent housing, showing that the number of homes renting for less than $600 a month declined by 450,000 units, while those renting above $1,000 increased by over 5 million. This was between 2012 and 2017. The problem is much worse now.

All this important new construction should be done while keeping the process as simple as possible. I'm serious.

CONTRACTS FOR TENANT-BASED VOUCHERS SHOULD BE LONG TERM

As discussed in the previous chapter, Ms. Yanira Cortes is worried that her Voucher might not be renewed if Congress does not appropriate enough money. So far appropriations have been adequate and all contracts for Vouchers have been renewed. Still, the situation is uncomfortable. The Budget Committees should be able to look at past experience and budget enough funds for long term renewals, while, at the same time, allocating funds for one year in the annual budget. It would help both tenants and owners to sleep better at night.

PROVIDE HOME OWNERSHIP INFORMATION TO VOUCHER HOLDERS, AS WELL AS THE RIGHT TO REMAIN IN RENTAL UNITS

During another interview in chapter 11, Ms. Sholanda Rivers brought up a very good idea. Ms. Rivers suggested that the Section 8 information package should include information about home ownership. I thought, "why not." President Biden is considering a down payment assistance program that would provide $15,000 tax credits to increase home ownership rates. Voucher recipients should know that if they start to earn more money, they could think about owning a home, one of the main ways to accumulate wealth. With the proper counseling, home ownership can be an excellent option. James Stockard, currently a lecturer at the Harvard School of Design, quoted a study that claimed that the average wealth for white families in the Boston area was about $250,000. For Black families the average wealth was $8.

Matthew Desmond, the famous author of Evicted, wrote an article in the New York Times Magazine in 2017 that claimed that "the average home owner boasts a net worth ($195,400) that is about 36 times that of the average renter ($5,400). At the same time former President Trump was advocating substantial cuts in the HUD budget.

Still, in project-based Section 8 buildings, many tenants whose incomes increase opt to stay in their buildings and their communities. Some pay the Fair Market Rent. They can become role models for other tenants, and valuable community leaders. Nevertheless, everyone should know about the possibility of owning a home

A LITTLE RESPECT FOR LANDLORDS

In the first years of Section 8, as described in chapter 5, Settlement Housing Fund invited the leaders of the Real Estate Board, the Community Housing Improvement Program, and the Rent Stabilization Association to a meeting. We wanted to encourage landlords' participation in the tenant-based program, and we needed to understand their issues. Many owners seemed interested. This was at a time when New York City was losing population, and some owners were experiencing vacancies. We teamed up with a technical organization called Interface and decided to develop a computerized data base where owners could list units available for Section 8 tenants. We obtained a grant to cover our costs, and the Housing Authority agreed to take over operations after a few years if we could demonstrate the program's success. We were quite successful indeed. Recently I found a very positive article from a landlords' publication, the <u>Real Estate Weekly</u>, October 18, 1976. The article claimed that our program was a "refreshing exception" to the tendency of "people who concern themselves with the problems of tenants to have a blatant disregard of the plight of property owners." We were able to satisfy the fears of the owners. In the early years of Section 8, the owners in New York were happy to accept Section 8 tenants. They even became advocates.

Today the situation is very different. Rents have indeed "gone through the roof." Tenants have 120 days to find an apartment, twice as long as in the early days. Still, many tenants seem unable to find owners who will accept them. Sometimes property owners just prefer to avoid lower income tenants. However, there are many cases that owners are struggling hard to stay afloat. These owners should not be reluctant to accept Section 8.

An op ed article in the March 12, 2016 edition of the New York Times by Bert Stratton is a case in point. It is entitled, "I'm Not Evil. I'm a Landlord." Mr. Stratton describes how he had to evict drug dealers as well as a man who sexually harassed his female neighbors. Stratton's typical rents ranged from $490 to $630 a month. He did accept at least one Section 8 tenant. He tried very hard to keep his small building in good repair, but his situation was far from easy. At least he had a sense of humor.

Even Donny Capa, the hairdresser I discussed in the introductory chapter, a guy who really likes the program, has dropped out from Section 8, at least temporarily. His first experiences had been excellent. If the inspector had a problem, he or she could fix it on the spot. One time one of Donny's carbon monoxide alarms was out of date and unacceptable. The inspector had a new one in his backpack, and helped Donny with installing it. Recently, however, there seem to be new requirements that Donny cannot meet, and the new inspector seems to enjoy saying "no."

Donny hopes things get better because it would be great to accept Section 8 tenants again.

In a memorandum from HUD's office of Inspector General, dated January 25, 2021, there was a description of potential incentives that could be offered to landlords. Several interesting ideas were suggested. Some of the incentives were monetary, including bonuses for new participants, property damage reimbursement, vacancy loss payments and a few others. Nonmonetary incentives included direct deposit of payments, landlord liaison and a streamlined inspection process. HUD did not follow through by adapting any incentives at all. Perhaps the Biden Administration will consider doing something.

In the meantime, State and local government agencies, together with housing advocates, should reach out to owners now to understand their reluctance to accept tenants with Vouchers. Some states enacted laws that prohibit landlords from rejecting tenants because of "sources of income," meaning Section 8. The law seems to be disregarded quite often. New York is one of the states experiencing problems. An article in the New York Times on March 19, 2021, reported that the Housing Rights Initiative has filed a lawsuit in New York, suing 88 brokerage firms and landlords that discriminate against tenants with Vouchers. The Community Housing Improvement Program, (CHIP), a landlords' group that originally supported the program and participated in the Settlement Housing Fund data bank, recently called Section 8 "a bureaucratic nightmare." This organization was not among the groups that were sued.

An article in the Wall Street Journal on March 20, 2021, claimed that "thousands of building owners across the country are rejecting the recent rental assistance provided in the Covid Relief Act".

If we want to go way back in history, the real estate industry opposed public housing in the 1930's, arguing that a housing allowance would be better because it would allow lower income families to live in private housing. We should be able to figure out a way that owners would accept Section 8 tenants willingly today.

This seems like the perfect time for city agencies or other organizations to convene a group of landlords to seek their input. The state housing agency in Rhode Island has initiated a program called "Hello Landlord." The program uses technology to reach out to landlords, accept suggestions, announce policies that aim to dispel landlords' fears, and more. The techniques range from face-to-face meetings to attractive videos that shine a positive light on Section 8. It would be worthwhile to see if "Hello Landlords" does, in fact, attract landlord participation. A landlord-friendly approach seems long overdue in many localities.

TENANTS DON'T HAVE AN EASY TIME NAVIGATING THE SYSTEM

It can be difficult for tenants too, especially in recent years because federal funding kept shrinking. Sadly, the New York City Housing Authority stopped taking new applications for Vouchers in December, 2009. There are about 35,000 applicants remaining on the Voucher waiting list. The income limit for a single person is $39,800, $45,500 for two people, $51,200 for a family of three and for a family of four, the limit is $56,850. In Boston, as cited by Desmond in 2017, applications for new Vouchers were halted in 2008. In Los Angeles, the average wait for a Voucher was 11 years.

The lucky tenant who has a Voucher must find an apartment with rents at or below the payment standards (Fair Market Rent). In January 2021 the standards in New York City were as follows:

0 Bedroom $1,900

1 Bedroom. $1,945

2 Bedrooms. $2,217

3 Bedrooms $2,805

4 Bedrooms. $3,006

This probably seems astronomical to people who remember rent levels twenty years ago. The pandemic did lower average rents. Still, in April,2021, the average rent in the five boroughs for a one bedroom unit was $2,500, according to a survey by Zumper. This was 16 per cent below the average in 2019, and significant increases are anticipated once the pandemic is over.

The tenant's application for Section 8 requires a social security number for the head of household and birthdays and documentation of income for other family members. There are also questions about employment, citizenship and health.

Once a family is accepted for a Voucher, eight steps are needed before paying rent. First is the Section 8 briefing. Next the applicant waits to receive a Voucher. He or she then has 120 days to find an apartment. (Not easy). As mentioned above, New York and other states have passed laws that prohibit discrimination because of "source of income," meaning Section 8. However, reports of discrimination are widespread. Indeed, tenants have to struggle very hard to find apartments within 120 days.

If the family opts for an apartment with a slightly higher rent, the family could pay up to 40 per cent of income for rent. (How could the family eat, I wonder).

The next step after finding an apartment is to submit the rather complicated landlord package to the New York City Housing Authority (NYCHA) or the New York City Department of Housing Preservation and Development (HPD). The City then checks the rent for compliance. The agency then sends an inspector to go through the unit. Sometimes appointments for inspection get missed. If the unit passes inspection, the tenant can move in. Finally, the Housing Assistance Payment Contract is signed, and the owner receives rent. These requirements are not unreasonable. However, inevitably appointments are postponed, or the inspector shows up on the wrong day. Tenants need to be persistent, and landlords need to be patient.

Although the process does not seem seriously onerous, in fact, I did not hear complaints from tenants. The huge issue is the reluctance of landlords to accept Section 8 tenants and the delays of inspections, contact signing, and payments, which can seem endless. Even worse, NYCHA, which provides assistance for over 85,000 tenants, has not accepted additional applicants for the last 12 years.

The Biden program could change everything.

HOW WOULD AN EXPANDED SECTION 8 PROGRAM BENEFIT SOCIETY?

Okay. I know. Section 8 will not cure the common cold. There will always be snafus. However, the benefits of the program to Voucher holders and to the public welfare could be significantly important, if combined with the development of enough affordable housing.

The New York Housing Conference just received notice that the Robin Hood Foundation will provide a grant for a study of the economic impact of affordable housing. I am very eager to read the results of the study.

For starters, if implemented correctly, the program could end homelessness. In order to do so, the development of supportive housing would be essential for many (but not all) homeless individuals and families. This will not happen overnight. It often takes a long time to develop supportive housing, especially because affordable sites are few and far between.

But if Section 8 is expanded, the first tenants to be assisted would be those who move into existing supportive housing or those who are ready for totally independent living. As the availability of Section 8 increases, the end of homelessness is conceivable.

Lauren Sandler, author of This Is All I Got, stated that "the cumulative effect of stable housing makes an exponential difference in positive outcomes over the lifetime of the family of a low-income tenant." Ms. Sandler spent a year with a young homeless mother who struggled with real bureaucratic nightmares, one after another. In order to get any of her benefits or even to apply for them, she would need to sit for hours, waiting for her turn to speak to a government official. She would miss work or her college classes. Often she would be told that she does not qualify for assistance because of one technical reason or another or to come back in a few weeks when applications might be ready. A Section 8 Voucher would have enabled this woman to stay in one place, send her son to the same school, year after year, develop academically and have the advantages that come from having a home, potentially ending a cycle of generational poverty.

It should be possible that with universal Section 8, homelessness would end within the next few years. That would not only eliminate the disgrace of homelessness in a very wealthy country. We would end up saving a lot of money because running homeless shelters cost at least twice as much as the operating costs of permanent affordable housing.

IS GOOD HOUSING GOOD FOR ONE'S HEALTH?

Yes. Certainly, bad housing is bad for one's health, as Jacob Riis famously documented in 1890.

Fast forward to 2021. According to Professor Megan Sandel, a MD/PHD at the Boston University School of Medicine, "A stable, decent, affordable home acts as a prescription for health, now and in the future. When you pair it with key educational and other supports, it becomes the platform for economic mobility for generations to come." Professor Sandel referred me to a study published in Health Affairs, (Vol.39, no,4). This was a study of a group that received housing assistance, compared to a control group. The study adds to the literature asserting that housing does lead to positive health benefits.

A number of other studies claim that good housing does have a positive association with health. One study from 2018 in "Science Direct" studied 341 U.S. rural children, ages 9 to 24 years. One of the major findings was that "Lower housing quality was associated with poorer psychological health initially and over time" other aspects of health deteriorated.

The interim report of HUD's Family Options Study, which looked at different interventions for homeless families, found that after 18 months, families who were offered a housing Voucher experienced significant reductions in subsequent homelessness, mobility, child separations, adult psychological distress, experience of intimate partner violence, school mobility among children and food insecurity after obtaining a Voucher." Is that all?

A study by the New York State Department of Health in May,2017, reported that "Homeless individuals use emergency departments and require hospitalization at rates three to four times higher than other citizens."

In Portland, Oregon, in 2014, The Center for Outcomes Research and Education, reported that "tenants in supportive housing had spent roughly $2,000 a month in health care costs, and once housed, the figure dropped to $899 a month, a 55% decrease."

According to an article by Will Fischer for the Center for Budget and Policy Priorities, Vouchers "for homeless families cut foster care placements by more than half, sharply reduced moves from one school to another, and cut rates of alcohol dependence, psychological distress, and domestic violence victimization among the adults with whom the children lived". Not bad.

A Los Angeles study found that providing housing for formerly homeless individuals resulted in significant savings in health care expenses; every dollar spent on housing saved $2 in the first year and $6 in subsequent years.

Other studies document positive effects of good housing on overall mental health, children's brain development, and limiting the spread of communicable diseases.

I'm always happy to read studies that prove what seems obvious. It's healthier to live in safe housing than on the streets or in overcrowded, substandard, vermin-infested residences.

SECTION 8 IS GETTING POPULAR

The headline of the New York Times' lead editorial by Jamelle Bouie on April 5, 2021 read, "Affordable Housing Should Be a Priority." The article went on to say that "any serious attempt to reduce inequality and increase workers' share of income has to make housing a priority."

In May, 2021, I attended a Zoom meeting with the two New York Senators and members of the New York Congressional delegation. It was organized by Rachel Fee, Executive Director of the New York Housing Conference. To my amazement, every speaker committed with enthusiasm and gusto to supporting Section 8 for every eligible household. "Housing is part of Infrastructure" was a rallying cry. This comes after decades of hearing that housing is not a national priority, followed by requests for realistic advocacy. This led me to beg the advocates to request what is needed, rather than trying to be "realistic." I usually said that compromise is inevitable, but we should at least start by trying for an optimum solution. We will know pretty soon whether Section 8 will be in fact expanded to meet the national need of low income households.

THINGS TO THINK ABOUT

If the Biden Administration is successful in obtaining Section 8 for all eligible households, it is urgent the localities have enough qualified staff to run the program effectively. It will be important to document tenants' incomes, hopefully by requiring a simple method of documentation. Scandals can undermine programs. If potential tenants lie about their qualifications, headlines will abound. At the same time, it will be important to use available funding expeditiously to help as many families as possible. If things go wrong, and they will, local officials should explain the problems truthfully and be prepared to outline steps for corrections.

Some pundits claim that government programs can never be efficient. I disagree. I was amazed, when I retired, to experience efficiency and smart, polite public officials when I registered to obtain Medicare and Social Security. Similarly, the Covid Vaccination sites in New York City were user-friendly and effective. Hopefully, the new Section 8 Program could become a similar model of excellence.

Even though universal Section 8 would dramatically improve the lives of low income tenants, other community development activities remain important. Access to healthy food, good education, and health care are essential. Job training should be offered as well. Planners are talking about "fifteen-minute neighborhoods," allowing residents to walk to work, shopping and amenities. Communities should be economically and ethnically integrated.

Universal Section 8, especially if available to all income groups who cannot find affordable housing, would be a wonderful start.

MS. FEE AND CONGRESSMAN JEFFRIES

I hope my readers will be inspired if I end this book by quoting an article by Rachel Fee and Congressman Hakeem Jeffries from the NY Daily News, February 13, 2021.

Americans "should begin by acknowledging housing is a human right rather than a political issue with funding levels subject to political infighting. Biden laid out a vision on the campaign trail in which every American eligible for Section 8 rental assistance would receive aid. This visionary proposal would substantially reduce the national poverty by moving 9 million people in the United States out of poverty, including 3 million out of deep poverty..." This action, with other programs, "would help usher in a new era in our history: one in which every American, no matter where they live, has access to an affordable home."

"Lamberg herself has played an impressive and award-winning role over the years as Executive Director of the Settlement Housing Fund in New York City and as a vocal campaigner for universal Section 8 to the current day. She modestly recounts her continued efforts to institute fair housing, including her work with the Manhattan Plaza project, which, in collaboration with Section 8 provisions, has helped innumerable aspiring actors as well as a host of elderly and other deserving segments of the population."

-Barbara Bamberger Scott
The US Review of Books

Housing Security:
A Section 8 Memoir
by Carol Lamberg

"A wealthy country like the United States should be able to provide acceptable shelter for all its residents."

Section 8 is a Federal housing program enacted by Congress in 1974 for the benefit of lower-income families. Author Lamberg took on a variety of administrative responsibilities in the long-term development of the program in New York City. She describes some of the difficulties inherent in its navigation, showing its growth and expansion over the past nearly fifty years. Lamberg notes that New York City has had a housing crisis since its earliest settlement, with housing regulations being established and then subsequently ignored.

**US Review** of Books

AUTHORS PRESS

CREATIVE BOOKS

In 1890, Jacob Riis wrote *How the Other Half Lives*, painting a disturbing portrait of the city's poverty-ridden slum dwellers and the corruption of its landlords and builders. Other pioneering voices included Governor Alfred Smith, Abraham Kazan, and U.S. Secretary of the Interior Harold L. Ickes. A major act of 1949 promoted "a decent home and suitable living environment for every American family," a goal that, Lamberg stresses, is still awaiting complete fulfillment. However, progress was made with President Johnson's creation of the Department of Housing and Urban Development (HUD). HUD's progress was temporarily slowed in 1972 when it was inexplicably put on a moratorium by President Nixon. Then came the needed comprehensive upgrade when President Ford signed the far-reaching Housing and Community Development Act, now generally known as Section 8. Even now, in re-reading it, Lamberg finds details of that act encouraging, promising realistic benefits to tenants and property owners alike.

Through the intervening years, complexities in the administration of Section 8 programs nationwide have inevitably arisen. Yet, the laudable aspects of the original vision remain, such as a commitment to explore solar energy. Lamberg herself has played an impressive and award-winning role over the years as Executive Director of the Settlement Housing Fund in New York City and as a vocal campaigner for universal Section 8 to the current day. She modestly recounts her continued efforts to institute fair housing, including her work with the Manhattan Plaza project, which, in collaboration with Section 8 provisions, has helped innumerable aspiring actors as well as a host of elderly and other deserving segments of the population.

She interviews a number of Section 8 participants, giving readers a broader view of her subject. Some of those interviewed report undeniable detriments in the system, such as sometimes being on a waiting list for years, problems with neglectful management, and some substandard conditions in the housing units themselves. Some speak of a general bias against those who live in Section 8 housing. Nonetheless, positive notes also ring through the tenant accounts, with Section 8 being seen as a much-needed stepping stone to further life achievement.

Through personal recollections and impressive data collection, Lamberg has diligently constructed this chronicle to better inform those with less direct knowledge of the issues she examines and urge those with awareness and influence to take a still closer look. She expresses her hope that the current administration will follow through on its campaign promise for every American to have access to Section 8 rental assistance. Anything less than that, she believes, is less than our American best.

Book review by:
Barbara Bamberger Scott
US Review of Books

Lightning Source UK Ltd.
Milton Keynes UK
UKHW012310290721
388013UK00001B/43